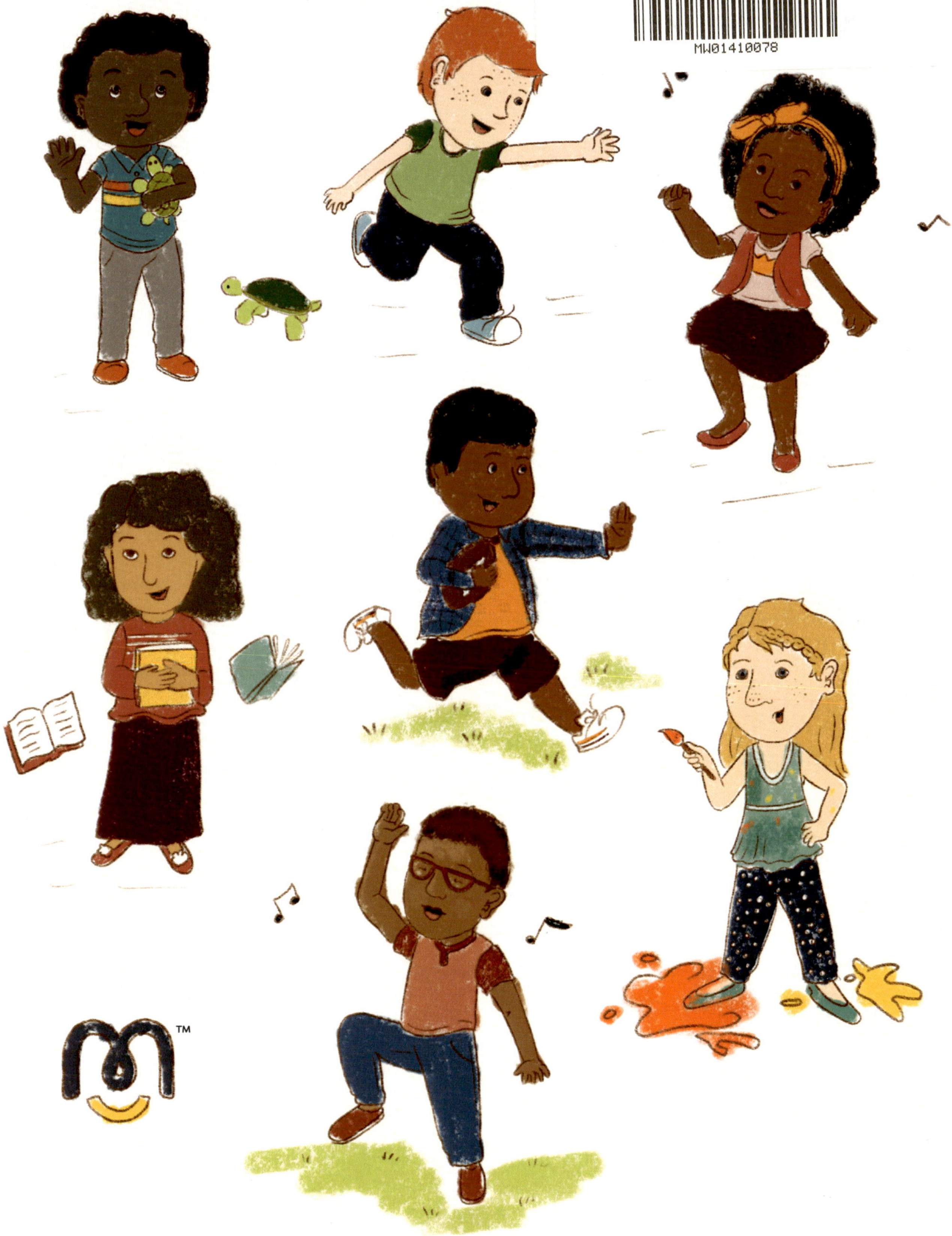

The **Sophia Day**™ Creative Team-
Kayla Pearson, Timothy Zowada,
Stephanie Strouse, Megan Johnson, Mel Sauder

Designed by Stephanie Strouse

© 2018 MVP Kids Media, LLC, **all** rights reserved

No part of this publication may be reproduced in whole or in part by any mechanical, photographic or electronic process, or in the form of any audio or video recording nor may it be stored in a retrieval system or transmitted in any form or by any means now known or hereafter invented or otherwise copied for public or private use without the written permission of MVP Kids Media, LLC. For more information regarding permission, visit our website at www.MVPKidsMedia.com.

Published and Distributed by MVP Kids Media, LLC
Mesa, Arizona, USA
Printed by RR Donnelley Asia Printing Solutions, Ltd
Dongguan City, Guangdong Province, China
DOM Aug 2018, Job # 03-004-01

helpme BECOME™

Becoming **Brave**
& Overcoming **Being Bullied**™

REAL mvpkids®

STOP BULLYING
S.T.A.N.D.
a 3-part series

STAND Up to Bullies™

SOPHIA DAY®

Written by Kayla Pearson   Illustrated by Timothy Zowada

TABLE OF CONTENTS

STORY	PAGE
Miriam's Birthday Party Bravery	1
Think & Talk About It	19
Liam's Bully Bug	21
Think & Talk About It	39
Yong's International Food Day	41
Think & Talk About It	59
MVP Kids® Character List	61
STA**ND** Pledge	63

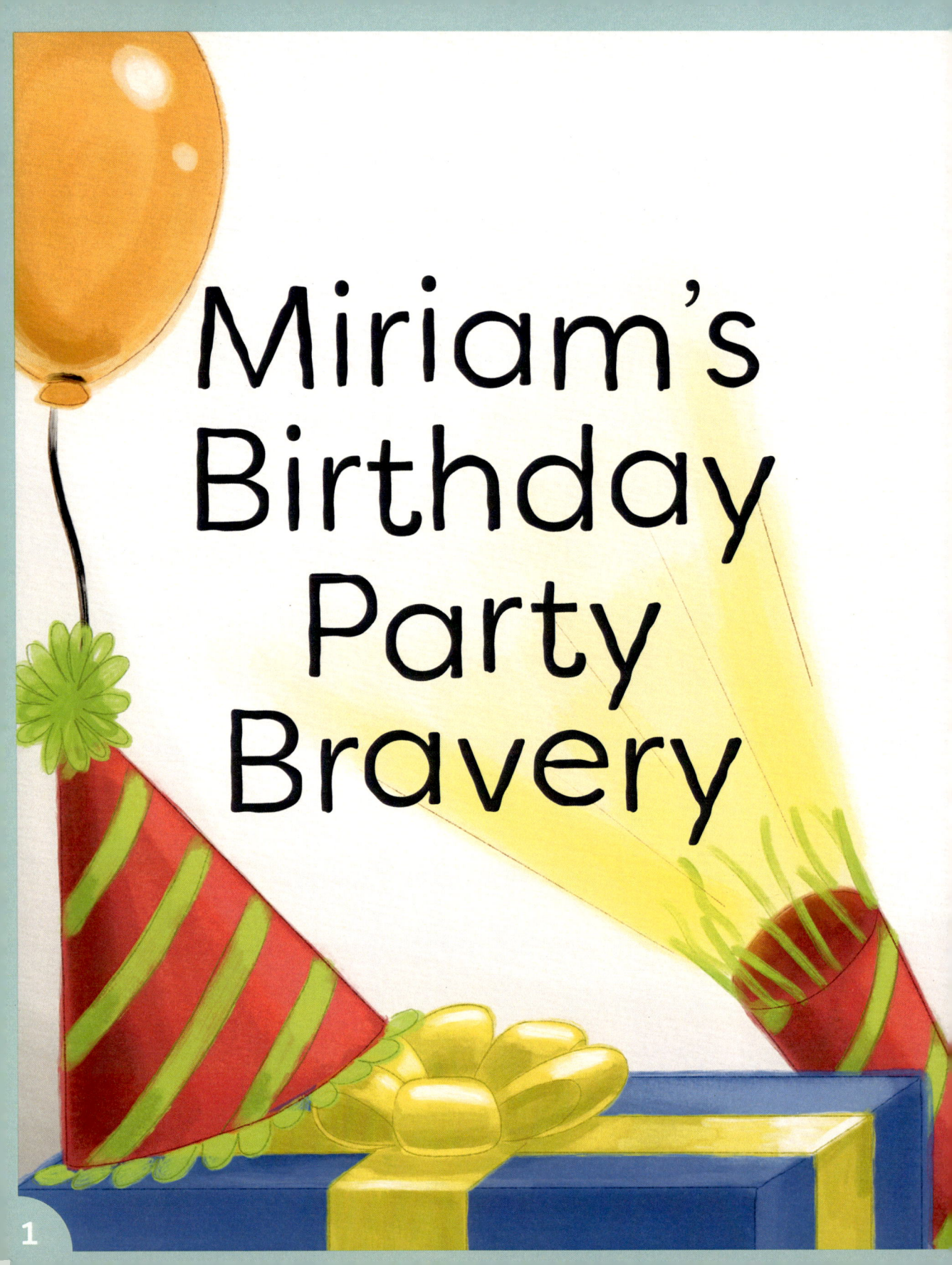

Miriam's Birthday Party Bravery

Miriam was excited to go to her friend's birthday party! She met Hannah at reading camp over the summer. They had fun reading stories together.

At camp, some girls bullied Miriam, because she was the youngest one there. They said mean things to her and tried to get the other kids to not play with her. **She worried** those girls would be at the birthday party, too.

Mama told her she didn't have to go if she didn't want to, but she promised Miriam she would be nearby if the girls were mean to her.

Her mom reminded her to

Stand tall and be confident.

Tell an adult if you run into trouble.

Act bravely and walk away if you need to.

Notice what is going on around you.

Display kindness when you can.

Miriam decided to be brave,
and go to the birthday party.

When Miriam arrived at the party,
Hannah greeted her with a hug.

"Happy Birthday!"
Miriam said.

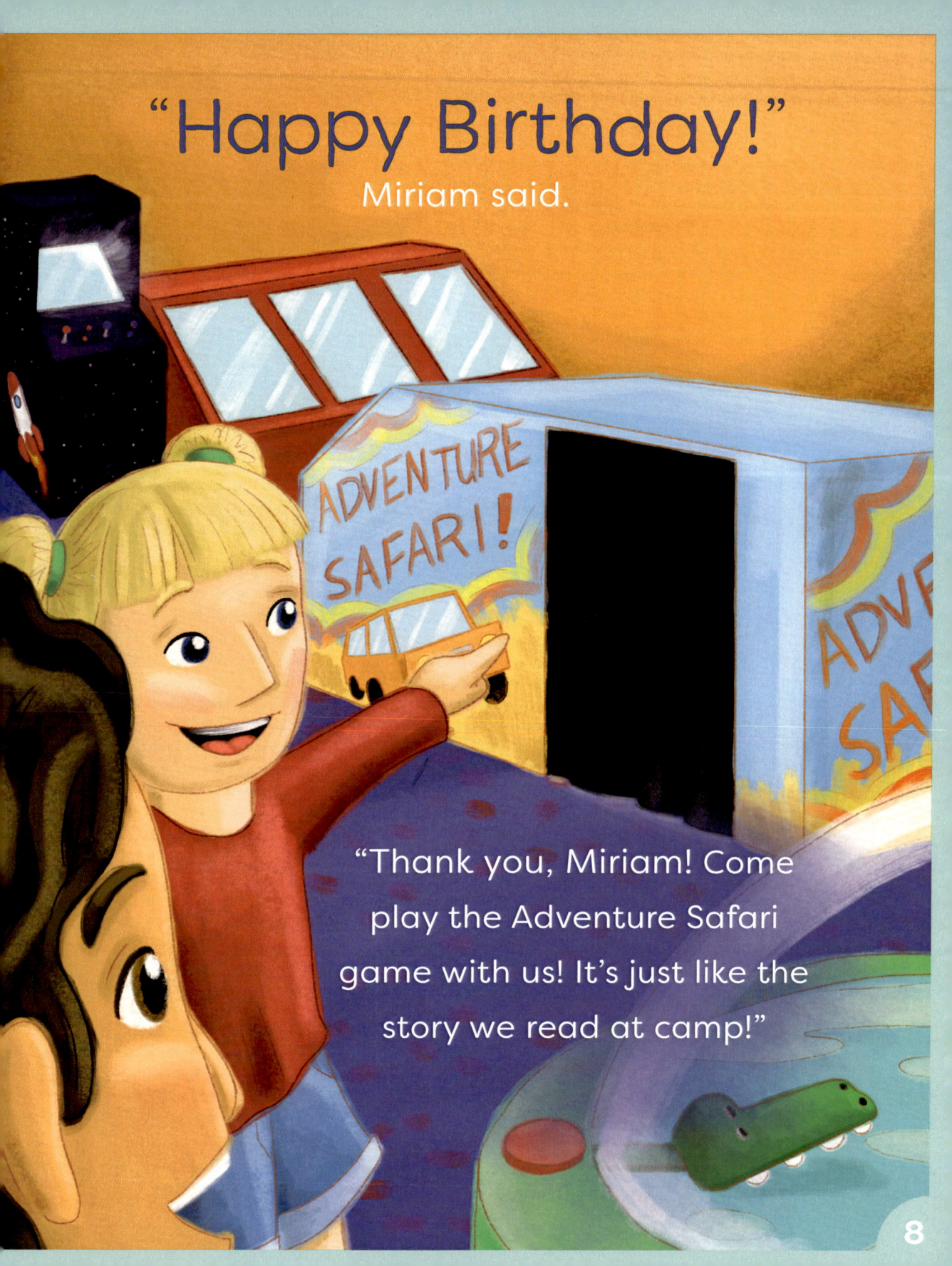

"Thank you, Miriam! Come play the Adventure Safari game with us! It's just like the story we read at camp!"

As they walked over to the game, Miriam **noticed** the other girls from camp.

"Oh no!" she thought. She wanted to be **brave** instead of showing the fear that was really inside her.

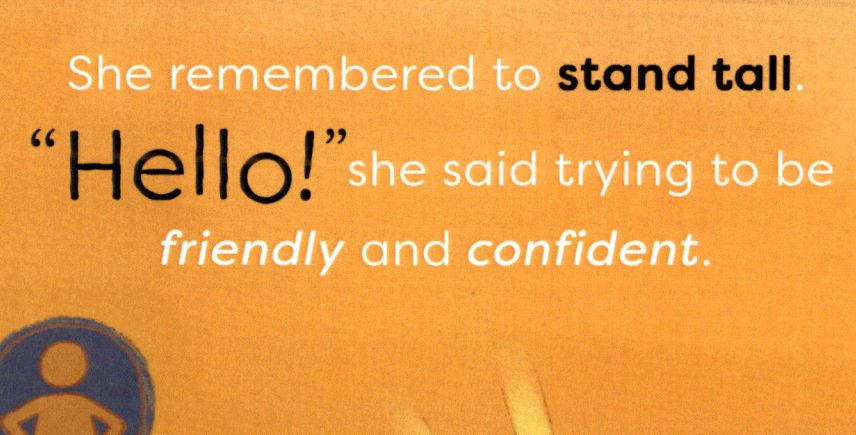

She remembered to **stand tall**.
"Hello!" she said trying to be *friendly* and *confident*.

The girls laughed at Miriam and said hurtful things to her.

Miriam took a deep breath to keep calm. "That looks like a fun game," she said **trying to be kind**.

"Little kids can't play that, it's a big kid game," said one of the girls.

Miriam could tell no matter how much she tried to be nice, these girls would just keep being mean. She decided she didn't want to be treated this way.

"Fine. I'll go play a different game."
Miriam walked away. She was upset that they were keeping her from playing the game with Hannah, but she knew walking away was wise.

She looked at some of the other games. As tears filled her eyes, she decided she just wanted to go home. Then she heard someone calling her name.

"**Miriam, wait!**" She turned around to see Hannah walking toward her. "I'm sorry they were mean to you. I told them if they were going to be mean to my friends, then I don't want to play with them."

"Thanks, Hannah."
Miriam wiped her eyes. She appreciated Hannah standing up for her.

"Let's go play the monkey game!" Hannah said as she grabbed her hand.

When the party was over, Miriam **told her** mom what happened. "I'm proud of you for **acting bravely and walking away**. I'm glad you have a good friend like Hannah who is **so kind** to you."

Miriam was glad, too.

THINK & TALK ABOUT IT

Miriam's Birthday Party Bravery

Discuss the story...

1. Why was Miriam worried about going to the birthday party?

2. How was Miriam brave when she saw the girls who bullied her at camp?

3. When the girls kept saying hurtful things, what did Miriam do?

4. How did Hannah display kindness to Miriam?

5. What ways did you see Miriam and Hannah taking a **STAND** against bullying?

Stand Confident | **Tell an Adult** | **Act Bravely & Walk Away** | **Notice Surroundings** | **Display Kindness**

Discuss how to apply the story...

1. What do you think it means to be brave?

2. What are some different ways kids bully other kids?

3. How do you feel when someone is bullying you?

4. How did you respond to the person bullying you?

5. What are some ways you think you can be brave?

FOR PARENTS & MENTORS: Encourage your child to come to you when encountering a bully. When a child does come to you with a bullying problem, be sure to first calmly listen so you understand what has happened. Make sure they understand that it is not their fault they are being bullied and they don't deserve to be treated disrespectfully. When possible, advise your child with peaceful ways to deal with the bullying problem on their own. However, if the bullying escalates or includes physical bullying, help your child by contacting the appropriate authorities right away.

Every bullying situation is different and can be handled in different ways. One peaceful way a child can deal with some bullying problems is by being brave and walking away. Often, responding defensively or aggressively can make matters worse. Simply walking away can diffuse a situation.

For additional tips and reference information, visit **www.realMVPkids.com**.

Liam's Bully Bug

"Liam! Are you ready to go to the park with us?" called Liam's dad.

Liam quickly grabbed his new bug kit and ran downstairs.

Liam stopped. He remembered the older boys who bullied other kids at the park. The boys would call kids names, make threats and push them around.

Liam wanted to be brave. He didn't want fear to stop him from enjoying his new bug kit.

Liam walked to the park with his family.
He noticed those kids were not around, so it was safe to play.

He pulled out his kit and started searching for bugs. "Wow! Look at the size of that beetle!" He examined the beetle with his magnifying glass.

Liam walked farther away from the playground as he searched the bushes and trees for bugs. He didn't notice the older boys walking toward him.

28

"Hey! What do you think you're doing?" Liam froze. His mind started racing for how to get away.

He tried to walk away, but the older boys blocked his way. He was stuck.

Then he remembered what his dad taught him when Liam **told his dad** about those kids.

"Hold back your anger and don't get upset. **Think of a bumblebee.** The more you swat at a bee, the more the bee will try to sting you. The same goes with bullying. The more upset you get, the more the bully will be mean to you."

"Do you want to see the bugs I found?" Liam asked trying to stand tall and be confident.

"Ew no! We don't want to see your stupid little bugs!"

"They're really cool. This one even has pinchers."

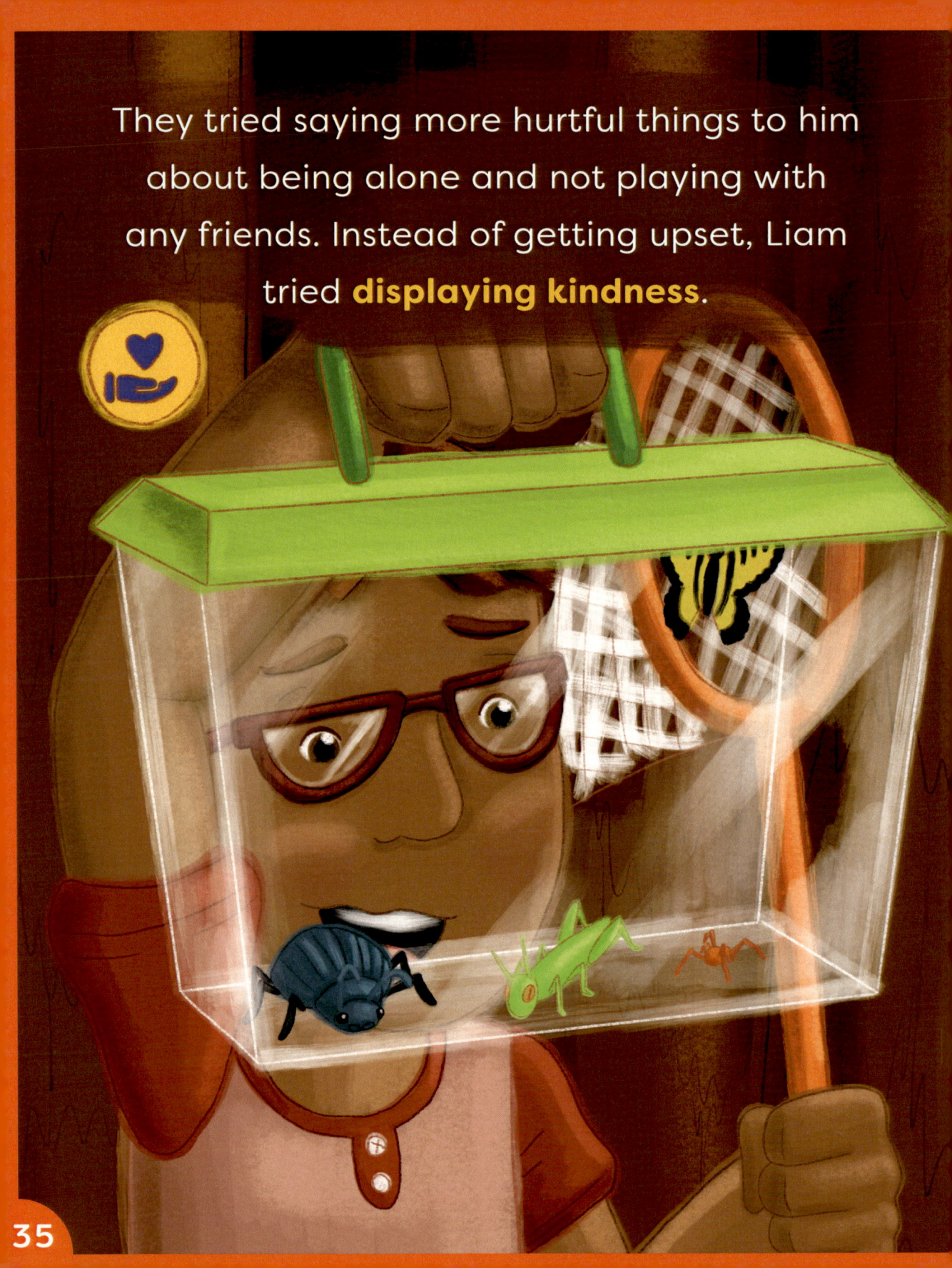

They tried saying more hurtful things to him about being alone and not playing with any friends. Instead of getting upset, Liam tried **displaying kindness**.

The boys weren't interested. "I'm tired of this. Let's go," said one of them. The boy grabbed Liam's bug kit and threw it on the ground as they walked away.

Liam quickly made sure the bugs were all right. He **wasn't** going to let those boys stop him from enjoying his bug kit.

Even if he was different from the other kids, Liam was going to **STAND tall**. Liam liked what he liked and Liam liked being himself.

THINK & TALK ABOUT IT

Liam's Bully Bug Experience

Discuss the story...

1. Why did Liam want to be brave?

2. How did the boys bully Liam?

3. What did Liam's dad teach him about responding to bullies?

4. Even though the other kids weren't interested in the same things as Liam, did that stop Liam from enjoying them? Why?

5. What ways did you see Liam taking a **STAND** against bullying?

Stand Confident | Tell an Adult | Act Bravely & Walk Away | Notice Surroundings | Display Kindness

Discuss how to apply the story...

1. What are some things you like to do?

2. Do you know others who like to do them, too?

3. Do you know kids who don't like what you like?

4. How does that make you feel?

5. Even though the other kids weren't interested in the same things as Liam, did Liam change what he liked to make the boys stop teasing him?

FOR PARENTS & MENTORS: When dealing with bullying situations, helping your child develop self-confidence is very important. Building confidence can be as simple as complimenting your child, especially when it comes to effort and work ethic. Teaching manners and respect of others has also proven to strengthen self-confidence. Another method is to give a child age appropriate responsibilities around the house that will give them a sense of accomplishment. Do what you can to help build up your child's self-esteem.

If there is a positive activity in which your child is interested, spend time supporting your child in that activity. This will help you see the specific strengths of your child. If possible, find other kids who are interested in the same activities and encourage your child to connect with them.

For additional tips and reference information, visit www.realMVPkids.com.

Yong's International Food Day

"Stop it, guys!"

Yong was tired of the bigger kids who bullied him at school. They would grab his lunch box and tease him about the food he ate.

That night at dinner, Yong's family was eating his favorite meal. "We made so much food tonight! We'll have enough leftovers for your lunch tomorrow, Yong," his mother said.

"Why can't I have lunches like all the other kids?!"

Yong threw his chopsticks and ran into his bedroom.

"Yong, what's wrong?" his dad asked.

"Kids at school always make fun of my lunches. **They are so mean!**" Yong **told his dad** about the bullies as he buried his head in his pillow.

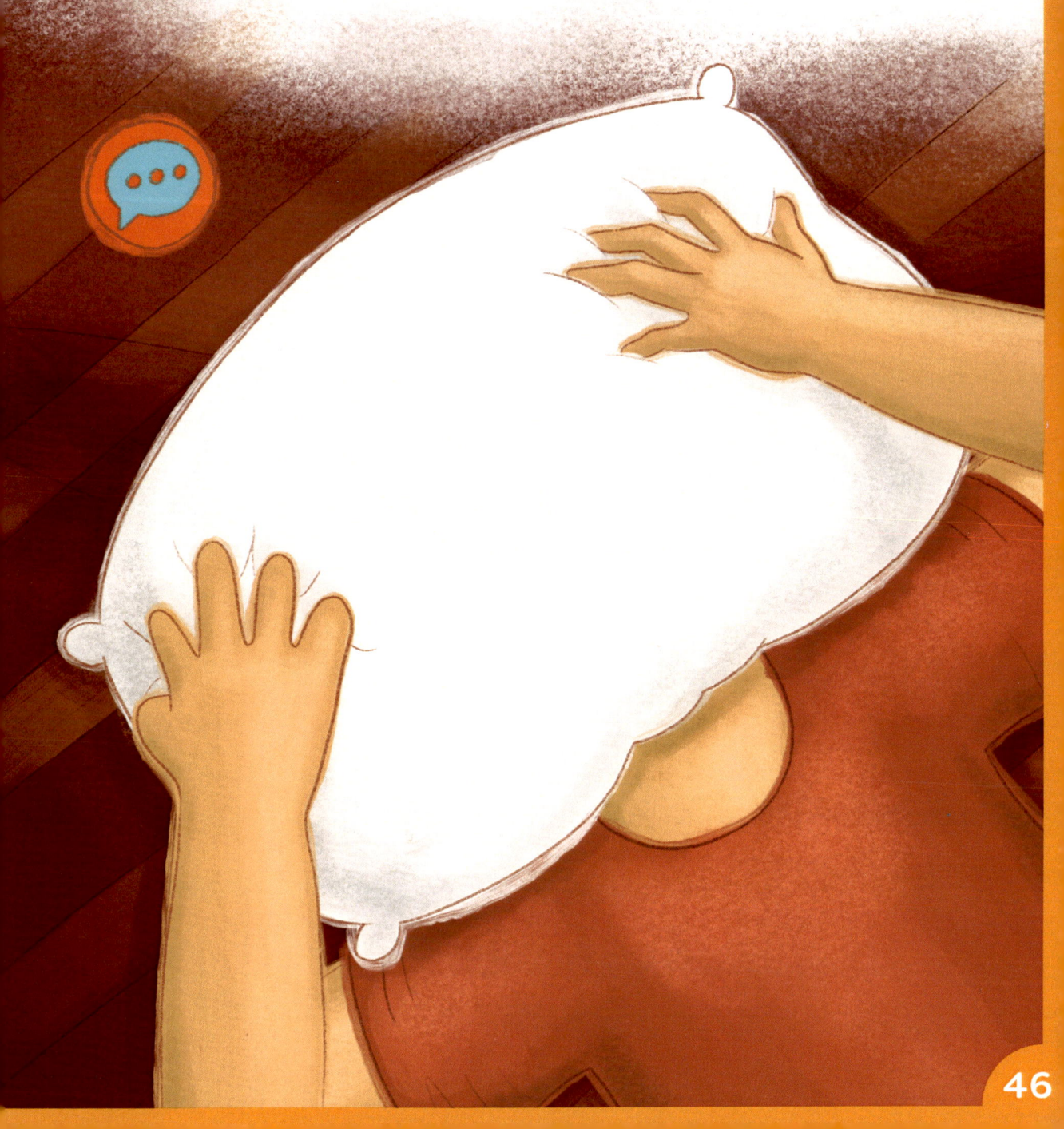

"I'm sorry to hear that, bâobâo*. When I was your age, I had kids pick on me, too. I would **stand tall**, act bravely and walk away. After a while, they left me alone."

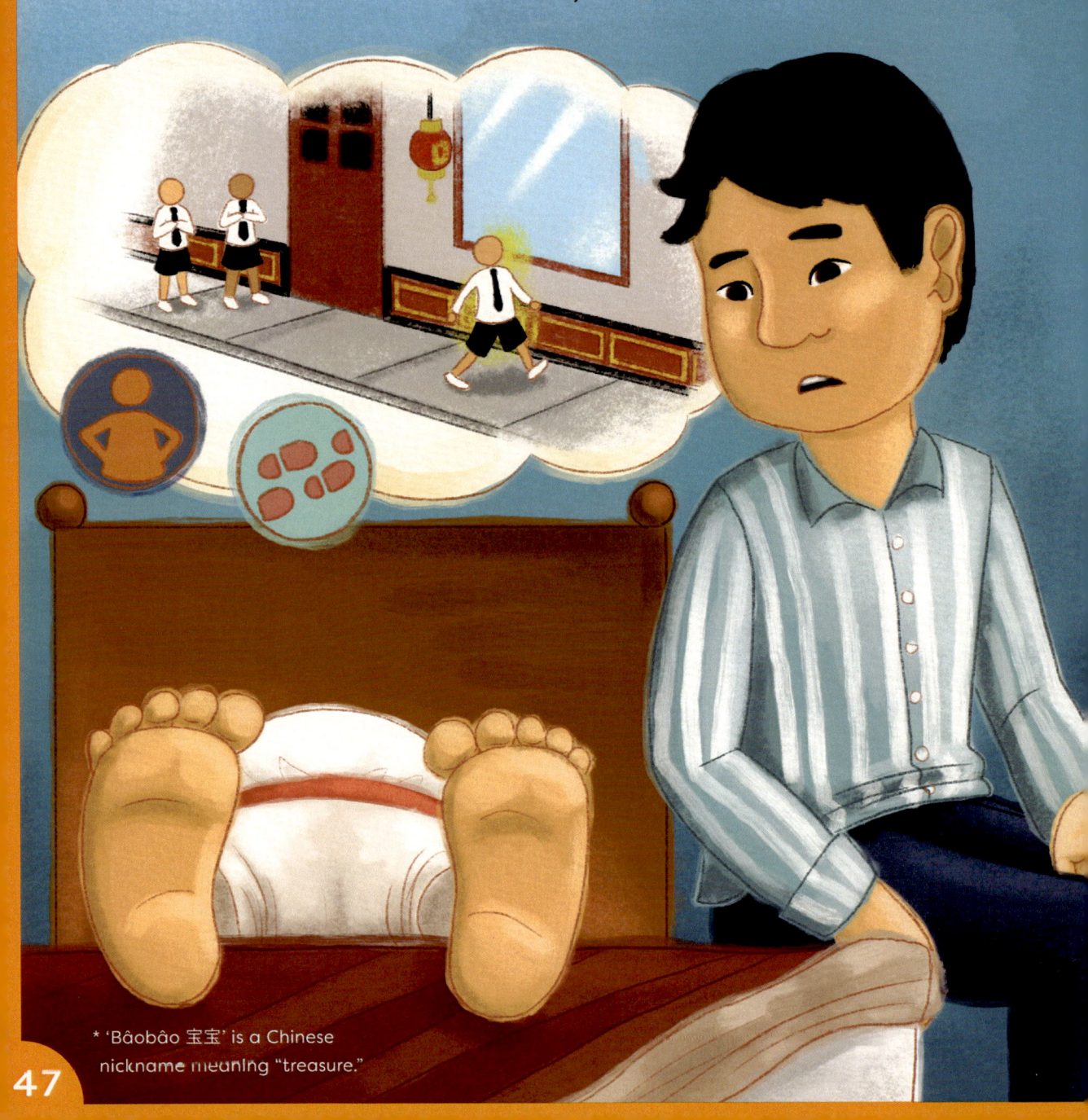

* 'Bâobâo 宝宝' is a Chinese nickname meaning "treasure."

"But dad, I've tried that and they just won't stop!" Yong said frustrated.

"I'm glad you told me. I will contact your teacher, so she can help you, too. I'm sorry you've been dealing with this."

49

Yong's dad continued, "One reason kids pick on others is because they don't understand those who are different. The boys at your school make fun of your food because they've probably never tried it."

"Yeah," Yong agreed. "If they tried Gong Gong's delicious food, they would understand."

Yong's dad talked to the teacher at his school and she agreed to help Yong. She had the idea of having an **international food party.** She contacted all the parents in Yong's class and asked them to bring a special dish to share with the class.

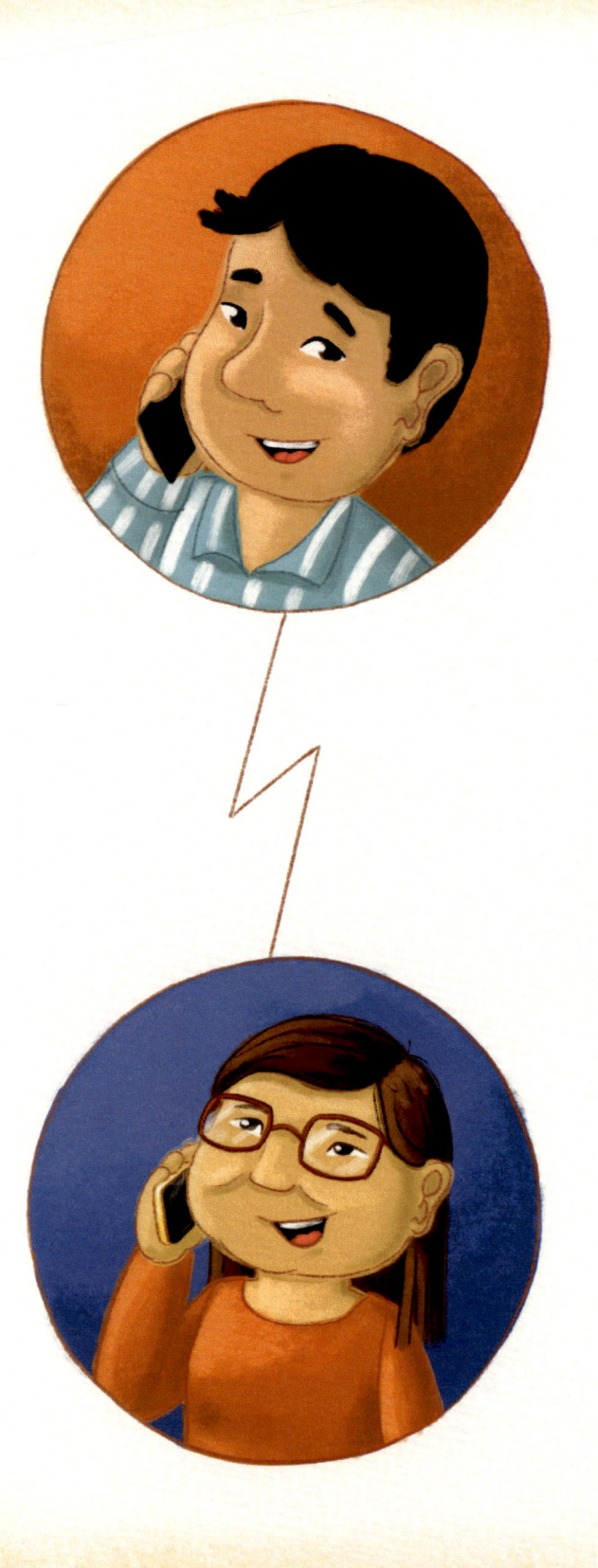

52

INTERNATIONAL FOOD DAY

The day for the international food party arrived, and Yong was nervous.

The kids had stopped bothering him since the teacher talked to them.

What if they tried his food and still didn't like it? What if they started making fun of him again?

Yong walked around and tasted a lot of **yummy** food from around the world.

When he looked back at his mom's table, he **noticed** Marcus and Anthony **about to try his food.**

When they took a bite, they really liked it! They even asked for more!

Later, Marcus and Anthony **displayed kindness** by apologizing to Yong.

"Yong, we're sorry we gave you such a hard time about your lunches," said Marcus.

"Yeah, this food is really good!" added Anthony.

Yong was glad his dad helped him find **a peaceful solution** to his bullying problem. From now on, he was going to **stand tall.**

THINK & TALK ABOUT IT

Yong's International Food Day

Discuss the story...

1. How did the kids bully Yong?

2. Why did Yong get upset at dinner?

3. How did Yong's dad stop the bullies when he was younger?

4. What happened when the kids who were bullying Yong finally tried his food?

5. What ways did you see Yong taking a **STAND** against bullying?

Stand Confident | **Tell an Adult** | **Act Bravely & Walk Away** | **Notice Surroundings** | **Display Kindness**

For additional tips and reference information, visit www.realMVPkids.com.

Discuss how to apply the story...

1. How does it make you feel when someone doesn't understand you?

2. Tell about a time when someone bullied you or someone you know for being different.

3. What is something about your culture that you like?

   The word "culture" refers to the foods, activities, holidays and beliefs that are important in different places around the world.

4. What could you learn by celebrating another culture?

5. What new culture would you like to experience? What ways could you experience it?

FOR PARENTS & MENTORS: Bullying can affect your child's behavior and personality. Signs your child is being bullied include depression, anxiety, decreased appetite, unexplained bruises or cuts, mood swings, nightmares and even becoming a bully. If you think your child is being bullied, help them know they can talk to you and that you want to help them. Listen to your child calmly and compassionately.

If the bullying is taking place at school, approach the child's teacher immediately. Schools have policies against bullying, and when the teacher is aware of the situation, they can help end the bullying problem with the help of principals, counselors or other school staff.
If your child is being bullied because of their race, children may feel shame and try to distance themselves from their family's cultures. Family heritage helps children with a sense of identity, so help your child feel pride in your family's background. Find ways to celebrate your culture in different community events.

Meet the

mvpkids®

featured in
STAND Up to Bullies™
with their families

MIRIAM NASSER

MRS. SALMA NASSER
"Mama"

LIAM JOHNSON

DR. MICHAEL JOHNSON
Father

ESME JOHNSON
Sister

AVA JOHNSON
Sister

YONG CHEN

HUANG CHEN
Father

LI CHEN
Mother

62

mvpkids

STAND against bullying!

Will YOU take a STAND to stop bullying?

Stand in front of a mirror and say the pledge aloud, then share with someone how you've decided to STAND against bullying.

I pledge to take a

S.T.A.N.D.

when faced with any bullying situation.

I promise that I will strive to...

Stand tall and be confident.

Tell an adult if I run into trouble.

Act bravely and walk away if I need to.

Notice what is going on around me.

Display kindness when I can.

*Note to kids, parents and mentors - Although everything in this book is copyrighted, you have our permission to copy this page for use in taking the pledge.

In a study conducted by StopBullying.gov, "about 49% of children in grades 4-12 reported being bullied by other students at school at least once during the past month, whereas 30.8% reported bullying others during that time."[1] From a very young age, we need to help our children understand and **STAND** against bullying.

―――――――

Do you need more resources and help regarding bullying? Please visit our website at
www.realMVPkids.com/stand-against-bullying/

The U.S. official government website can be found at
www.stopbullying.gov/

---

[1] "Facts About Bullying." StopBullying.gov, www.stopbullying.gov/media/facts/index.html.

Don't miss out on our 3-part **STAND** anti-bullying series!

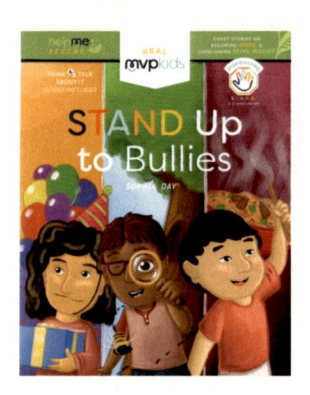

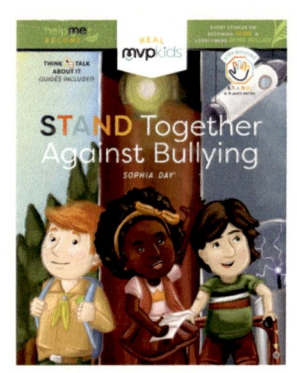

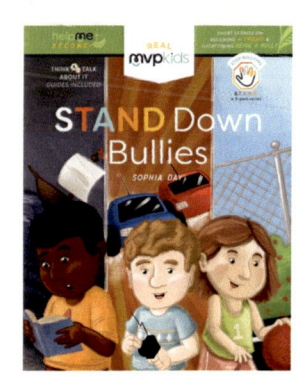

Grow up with our **mvpkids**

CELEBRATE! A **Preschool** Series
Ages 0-6

Our board books for toddlers and preschoolers focus on social, emotional, educational and physical needs. Helpful Teaching Tips are included in each book to equip parents to guide their children deeper into subject of the book.

help me BECOME
Early-Elementary
Ages 4-10

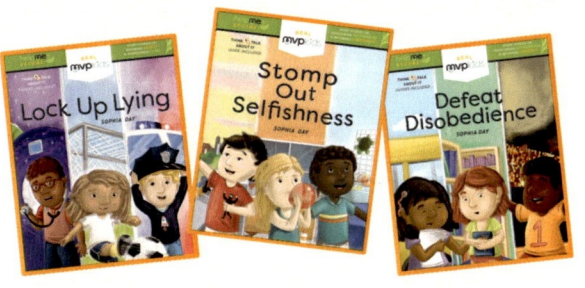

Our Help Me Become™ series for early elementary readers tells three short stories of our MVP Kids® inspiring character growth. The stories each conclude with a discussion guide to help the child process the story and apply the concepts.

help me UNDERSTAND
Elementary
Ages 6-12

Our Help Me Understand™ series for elementary readers shares the stories of our MVP Kids® learning to understand a specific emotion. Readers will gain tools to take responsibility for their own emotions and develop healthy relationships.

66

YONG CHEN
LEO RUSSO
FRANKIE RUSSO
JULIA ROJAS
GABBY GONZALEZ
AANYA PATEL
ANNIE JAMES
BLAKE JAMES
SARAH COHEN-GOLDSTEIN

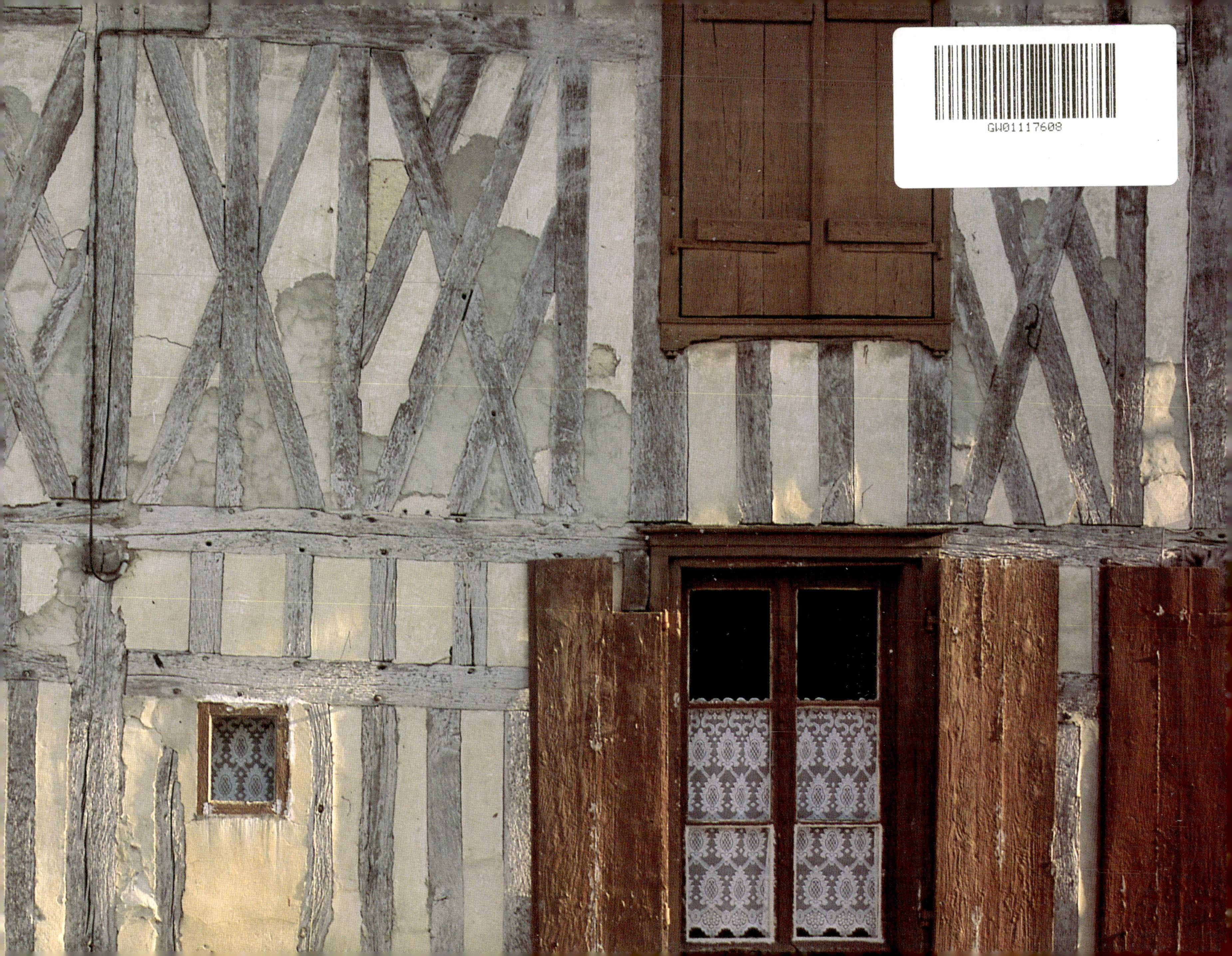

FRENCH FARMHOUSES AND COTTAGES

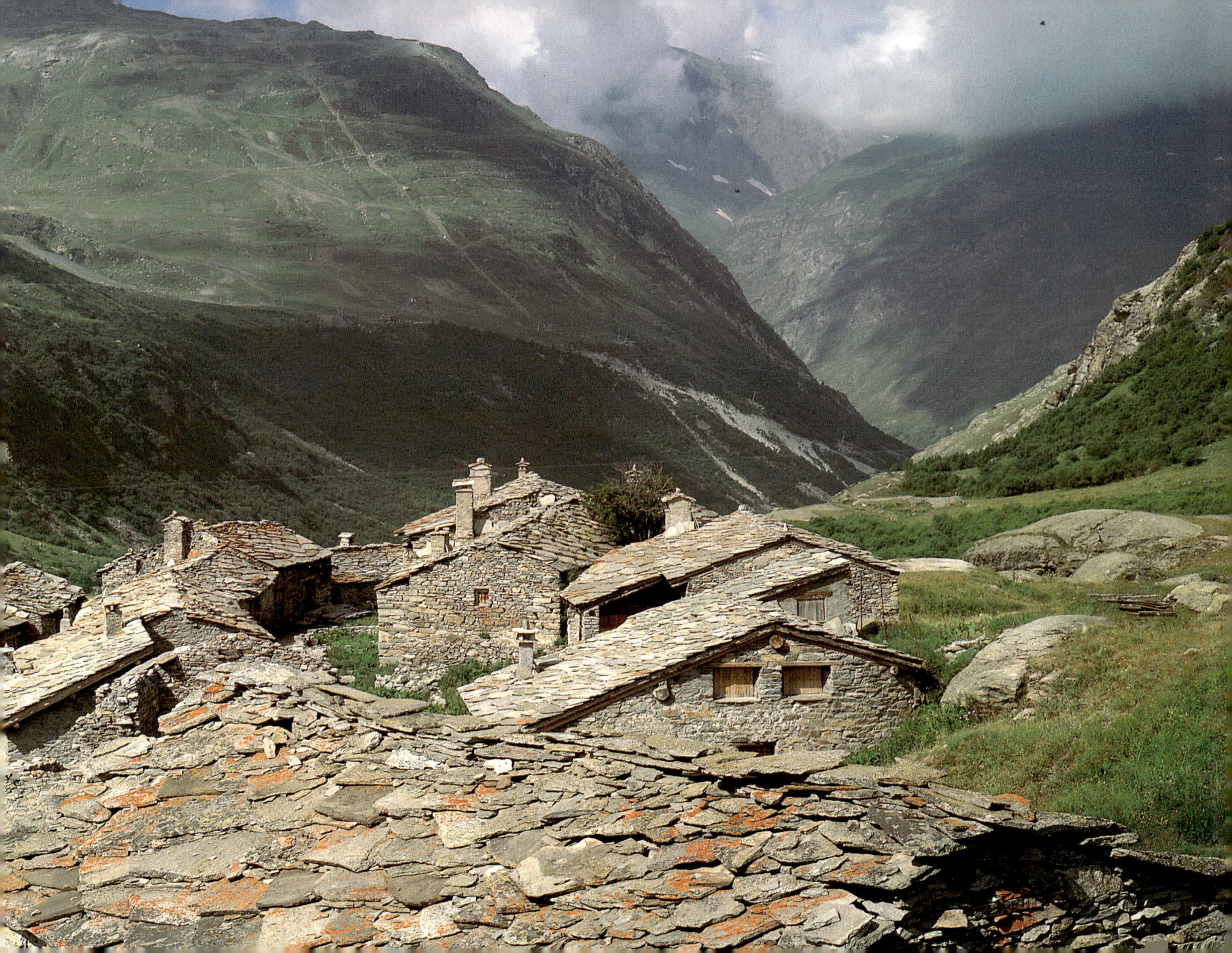

FRENCH FARMHOUSES AND COTTAGES

Text by Paul Walshe
Photographs by John Miller

Weidenfeld & Nicolson
London

Text © Paul Walshe 1992
Photographs © Weidenfeld & Nicolson 1992
First published in 1992 by
Geerge Weidenfeld & Nicolson Limited
91 Clapham High Street, London SW4 7TA

All rights reserved. No part of this publication may be
reproduced, stored in a retrieval system, or transmitted in any
form or by any means, electronic, mechanical or otherwise,
without the prior permission in writing of the copyright owners.

British Library Cataloguing-in-Publication Data
A catalogue record for this book is available from the British Library.

Typeset at The Spartan Press Ltd, Lymington, Hants
Printed and bound in Italy

Endpapers: Lesmont, Aube, Champagne-Ardenne (see p. 50)
Half-title page: La Chapelle d'Abondance, Haute-Savoie, Savoy
Title page: L'Ecot, Savoie, Savoy (see pp. 84–5)

Contents

Maps	6
Introduction	9
The Houses	38
Glossary	156
Bibliography	157
Author's Acknowledgements	158
Index	159

MAP OF HOUSE LOCATIONS

MAP OF HOUSE LOCATIONS

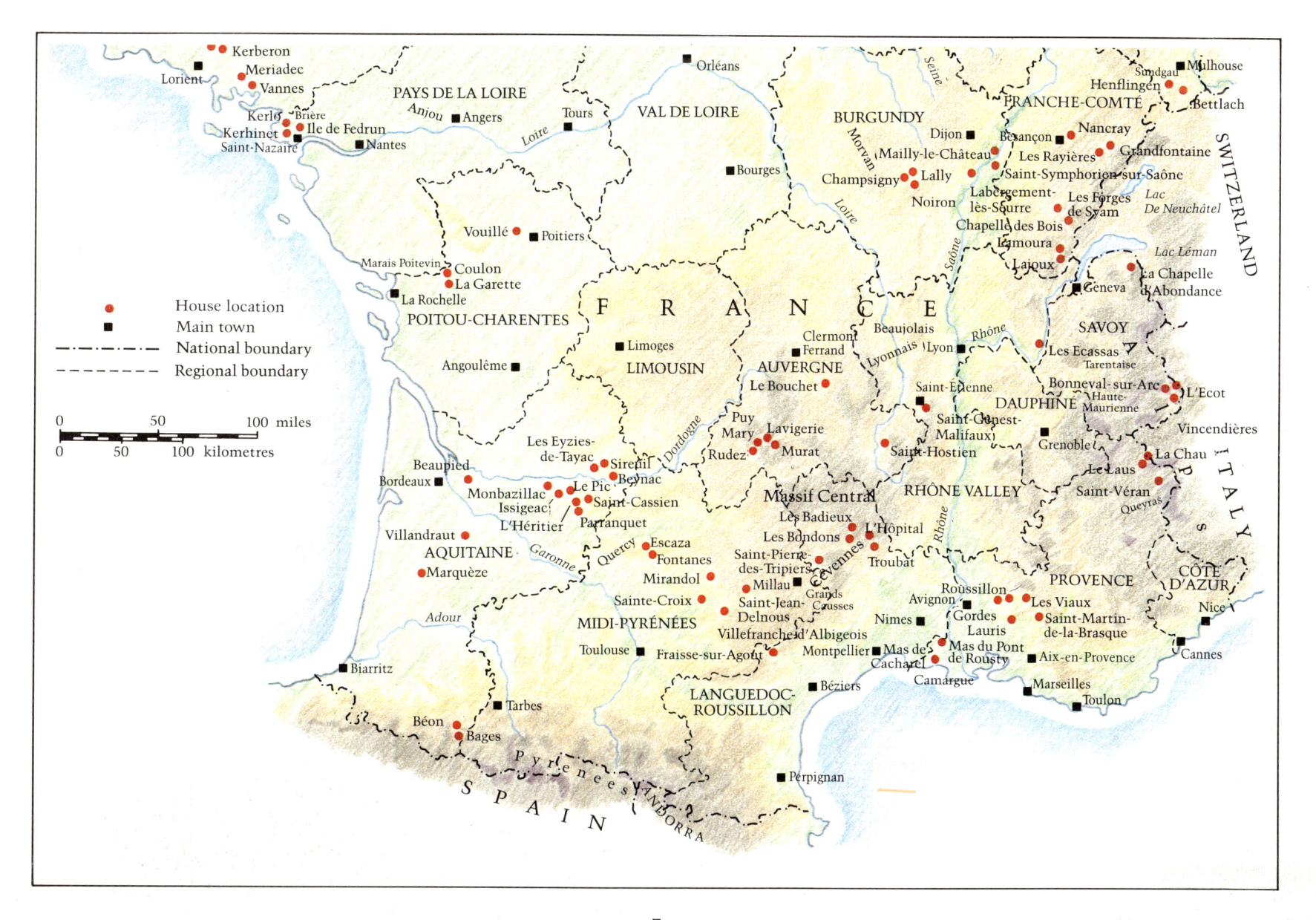

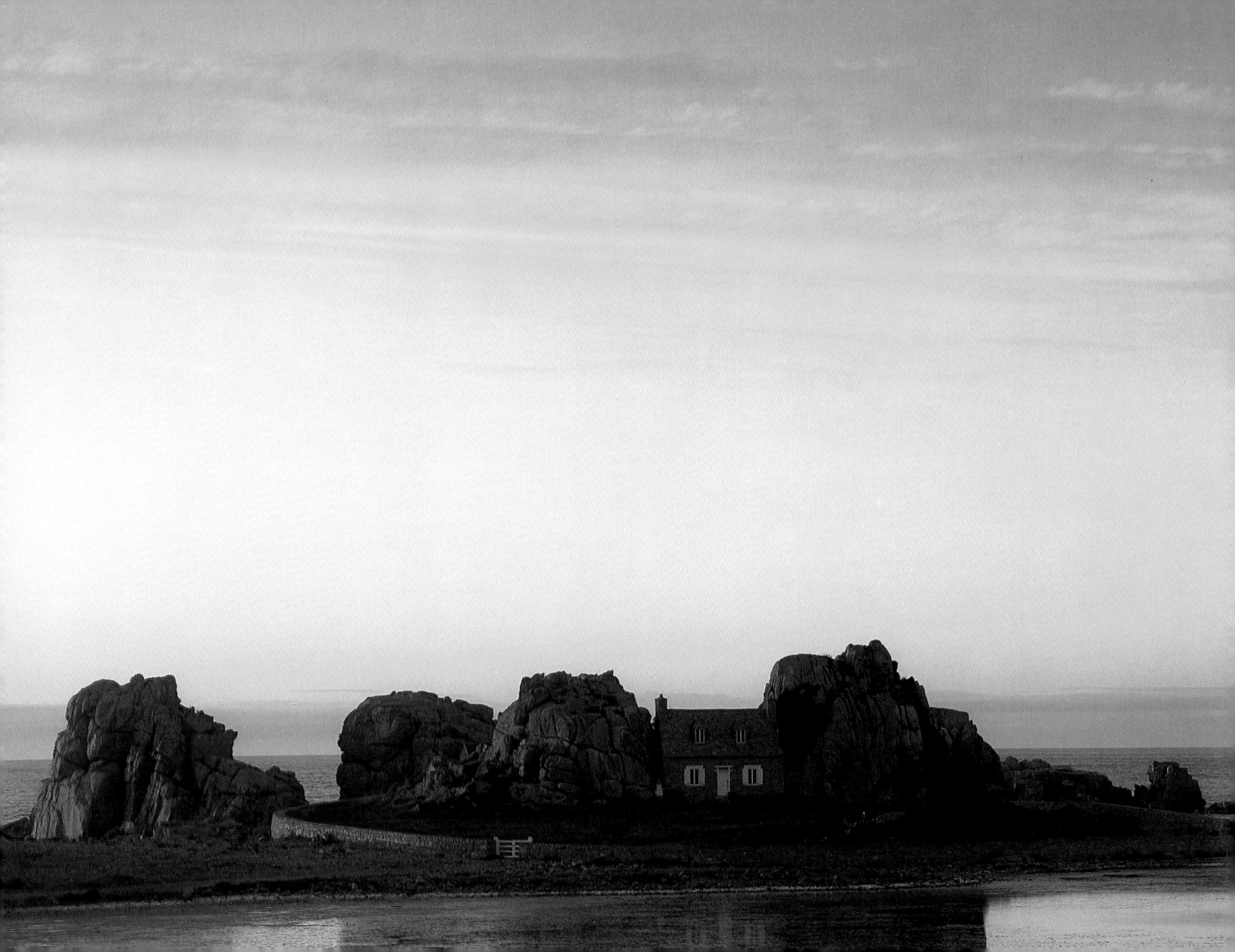

Introduction

**Plougrescant
Côtes-du-Nord**

A fisherman's *penty*, or cottage, shelters between outcrops of rose-pink granite on the Côte de Granit Rosé at Plougrescant in Brittany. The prefix *plou* is the Breton Celtic word for a parish (Welsh *plwyt*, Cornish *ply*), defined as the area which a priest could visit and administer and which people could reasonably cross to get to church on Sundays and Holy Days. Christianity overlaid a long pagan tradition, and parishes reflected the longer established *pays*, a word derived from the Gallo–Roman *pagus* meaning an area with its own identity. The modern administrative unit, the commune, of which there are 36,300 in France, is based on and originally coincided with these ancient parishes and *pays*. After the French Revolution parish units decreased in size as populations grew, settlements increased and hamlets once served by a chapel became parishes in their own right, although the average size of a commune in Brittany (now 26 sq.km/10 sq.miles), with its great expanses of unpopulated forest and heath, was always larger than that for the rest of France.

A peasant on foot, sitting astride his heavy horse or leading his team of oxen could reasonably travel 5 to 10 kilometres (3–6 miles) to market. As a result a pattern of *bourgs*, or market towns, each 15 kilometres (10 miles) or so from the next, has been laid down over the length and breadth of France. The stretch of country between these market towns was the peasant's world, his *pays*. Wars might take him from it and frequently neglect to return him; the need to find work, or a wife, might prise him away from it for a while, but only with the greatest reluctance would he move out of it. The *pays* explains France, it is France. The *pays* explains why the diversity of France is so much more than merely geographical. Every 30 or 40 kilometres (20–25 miles) brings a change of landscape, of patterns of settlement and farming; of flora, fauna, livestock; of folklore, custom and costume; of dialect and even of language.

The farmhouses and rural buildings of France exhibit an extraordinary diversity and variety simply because they are physical expressions of the relationship between man and nature, which is unique to each *pays*. They have encompassed and given form to the way people chose to live together, to work their land, ply their trades and crafts, bring up their children. They were products of local states of technology, local responses to climate, geology and geography, and local uses of the natural resources of wood and water, soil and sun. To the traveller they signalled departure from one *pays* and arrival in another. They also reflected the cultural and historical inheritance of a *pays*, because they were constructed out of patterns of thinking and ways of seeing and acting laid down long ago when men ceased their nomadic existence, settled down, looked about them and made the most of what they found.

The key to French rural vernacular architecture is therefore the *pays*, which was serviced by the *bourg* and in turn sustained the *bourg*. The *bourg* was the local centre for administration, justice and trade, providing a link to the outside world. Typically a *bourg* developed at the entrance or exit to a valley, at a cross-roads or on the edge of two *pays* producing different goods. Impenetrable forests and deep valleys, strong-running rivers and mountain ridges were its limiting factors. The market, shared by all the villages within its influence was its life blood, the market square its heart. On market days and fair days it would come alive to the squeal and mingle, the tumble and confusion, the noise and the gaiety of farmcarts and livestock, merchants and hucksters, wagons and gigs. But the *bourg* was still, for the peasant, the edge of his *pays*. At the end of that market day an easy gait would lead him home, and home for the French peasant was the village. This was the centre of his *pays*.

The village and the farmstead

The village, whether the clustered settlement north of the line between Saint-Malo and Geneva, so often considered to be significant in France, or the dispersed community south of it, was the basic unit of the French countryside, where the majority of farmhouses and rural buildings would be found. There were isolated farms such as the *granges, mas* or *bastides* of Provence, the great courtyarded farms on the cereal plains of the Île-de-France and Picardy, and the farms within the hedged fields of the Armorican massif in Brittany, but these were exceptions to the rule.

That so many of these farms and villages remain is an accident of French history. While in Britain a farm is usually an isolated unit in the countryside, lived in by a professional, full-time farmer working for profit, in France, certainly till 1945, a farm was part of a largely self-sufficient community which survived by doing all kinds of work including the working of the land. The only cash profit it needed to make was in order to pay taxes and seigneurial dues. The reason for this difference lay in the agricultural and industrial revolutions that took place in Britain in the eighteenth and nineteenth centuries. There the village-based peasant economy, with its shared open fields and commons, was destroyed by the enclosure of common land between 1750 and 1850. This resulted in the disappearance of the peasant farmer and the emergence of a new class of wage-earning labourer who had little or no direct interest in the land. By becoming wage earners, farm labourers lost their status and the whole character of British villages was changed. The improvements in agriculture which flowed from this agricultural revolution helped to bring into being an industrial society, which, between 1850 and 1900, moved the centre of gravity from the countryside to the towns and cities and forced the countryside to adapt to its needs and become transformed by its innovations. Badly paid and with his grip on the land loosened, the new wage-earning labourer could not resist the gravitational pull of the town, and between 1801 and 1911 the proportion of the population living in urban areas rose from 20 to 80 per cent.

No such fundamental structural change over a comparatively short period of time affected the French countryside. The beginnings of a similar enclosure movement under the *Ancien Régime* were halted by the Revolution, and when it did occur the change was gradual enough to be assimilated. As a result a village-based peasant economy has lasted well into the present century and even up to the present day. Certainly the farmhouses and farm buildings still to be found in these villages are the physical expression of a farming system and a way of life that have hardly altered in centuries.

Farm buildings generally clustered in villages because the village concentrated the means of survival, and survival could rarely be achieved solely by working the land. Every man in France whether he lived in the town or the countryside was always part-farmer, part-tradesman. Indeed, until the mid-nineteenth century townspeople used to abandon their trades every year in order to help with the harvest. The land was close to everyone and all were preoccupied by the state of the weather: early frosts that might destroy emerging fruit buds, heavy rains that might destroy a hay crop or cereal harvest, too much sun or too little sun, too much rain or too little rain.

In the villages of the countryside it was hard to distinguish between farmers who also practised a craft or trade and craftsmen or tradesmen who were also farmers. Men and women needed to do both in the interests of their own survival and the self-sufficiency of the village. Each village therefore had its skilled artisans like the wheelwright, the sawyer, the clog-maker, the mason, the carpenter and the blacksmith. Beside these everyday occupations some villagers made more specialized contributions to the autonomy of the community, like the man who could both recognize and deal with tape worm in pigs or the person who knew the healing properties of plants.

Villagers looked to each other and their land for their means of survival, but when they were unable to produce enough from the village lands to feed their herds and flocks, they would take them on local or long migrations to the high summer pastures of the Alps, the Vosges, the Massif Central and the Pyrenees, where they might stay till autumn. Even so villages would often have to travel out of their *pays* to look for seasonal work. The French proverb, *Noël avec les vieux, Pâques où tu veux* ('Christmas at home, Easter we'll roam'), suggests this was a common necessity. As Fernand Braudel wrote in *The Identity of France*, to which this section is indebted for its explanation of the rural structure of France, 'departures and returns brought desperately needed relief to the community of origin: departures because they reduced the number of mouths to feed, returns because they brought home cash savings, necessary for taxes, for unavoidable purchases and for the refloating of many Lilliputian smallholdings.' But the village remained the peasant's home and he unfailingly returned to it.

INTRODUCTION

The working of the village land

Each village occupied a particular area called the *finage*, which usually covered about 1000 hectares (2,500 acres). It comprised three concentric zones of management with the village at the centre. The logic determining the management of these zones was simply a function of the practical difficulties created by distance. It made sense to have the poorest lands, requiring the least attention, at the edge of the *finage*. Conversely it was a good idea to have the best land nearest the village. The better soil would allow more frequent crop rotations and proximity to the village would allow the plants to be well tended. Hence the location of villages at the centre of the best land and their bunching, as in Lorraine, so that as little of this land as possible was built over.

The better land thus comprised the inner and middle zones. A belt of kitchen gardens, hemp-patches and orchards surrounded the village, with beyond it a continuous circle of arable land, divided into different areas where crops were sown according to an accepted system of rotation – triennial (wheat or rye one year, oats or barley the second and fallow the third) in the north, biennial (cultivated one year, fallow the next) in the south. As with every rule in France there were of course exceptions, and as better access was gained to markets during the late nineteenth century and the peasant farmer began to produce a surplus for sale, specialization and monocultures – from wine to cereal production – increasingly found a place in the French countryside.

Common rights of grazing called *vaine pâture* in the north and *compascuité* in the south were held by the villagers and were essential to the keeping of livestock. These rights meant that grazing was permitted on stubble after harvesting, on fallow land as soon as the first grass appeared in spring, and on meadows as soon as the grass had started to grow again after haymaking. It also meant that the poor man's cow could graze the village green and the roadside verges. *Vaine pâture* was constantly under attack from rich and innovative landlords who saw it as an obstruction to increased productivity. But it withstood these attacks, in spite of regional edicts, until suppressed by law on 12 November 1889, amid an outcry from eight thousand communes. Even so it lingered on well into this century, another example of the innate conservatism of the French peasant and his stubborn insistence on doing things in the traditional way, whatever edicts might be enacted regionally or nationally.

Beyond the cultivated land lay the third and often largest zone, an uncultivated area which could include the remnants – vineyards and fruit trees, hedges and hedgerow trees – of past abandoned cultivation. It also contained untamed wilderness –

marshland and thicket, scrub and heathland, mountain and moorland and last but not least forest. All this apparent wasteland was actually an essential and integral part of the farming system, for every member of the village, from the poorest to the richest, enjoyed the right to graze cattle on it and the right to collect fuel, animal feed and fertilizer from it.

This carefully worked-out system of land management and the self-sufficiency that went with it emphasized the isolation of village communities, so encouraging the development of distinct and separate identities, which became concentrated over time as the factors that controlled it remained the same. For centuries – indeed until the last forty years – this constancy of routine and structure lay at the heart of the French countryside. Within these still seas, the *pays*, there were laid down, like geological strata, forms of vernacular architecture that were precisely tailored to fit these different ways of life.

Planning the farmstead

At the end of the First World War the architectural historian Albert Demangeon stood amidst the wreckage of some of these farm buildings and considered how best to approach their reconstruction. In his article *L'Habitation rurale en France*, from which the following section on the farm plan is largely drawn, he recounted how some theorists viewed this as an opportunity to introduce new principles into rural architecture, even importing fresh ideas from foreign countries. This Demangeon considered a grave mistake. What the peasant wanted, he believed, was his old house back – enlarged and better looking perhaps, healthier no doubt but built according to the principles of the past and the tried and tested customs of their rural way of life. To him the soul of a French farm building lay in its plan. It was here that the originality of French vernacular architecture lay. It might evolve over time, change shape and proportion to provide more air, more light, more comfort or more means of earning a living apart from farming; the furniture, tools and machinery it held might change, the materials with which it was constructed might develop and improve; but that basic, traditional plan remained.

The plan was fundamental because it established the peasant's relationship with his animals and goods. The nature of that relationship was always physically close, although the degree of proximity would vary from one region to another. Sometimes

Kerlo
Loire-Atlantique

Together with other villages in the parish of Saint-Lyphard in southern Brittany, Kerlo differs from the rest of the Brière region (see p. 138) in two respects. Its granite-built cottages were not whitewashed and its villages were not built to a circular plan on islands of higher land, but here as elsewhere the Briéron peasant lived in one simple ground-floor room. The furniture placed on its hard clay floor consisted of a wardrobe, beds, a bread bin and a table with benches down both sides. Above the fireplace was a timber mantlepiece with a dresser on it while set at right angles to the hearth were a couple of chests used as seats called *billots*. The smoke-blackened joists holding up the *grenier* above, where food was stored, and the rafters above that, were often made from *mortas*. These were exceptionally hard tree trunks dug up from the peat and marine clay deposited in the area when the sea rose in about 2700 BC.

there was complete cohabitation with not even a simple screen to separate man and beast, as was the case in certain Breton thatched cottages and winter quarters in the Hautes-Alpes. Variations elsewhere included putting living and animal quarters under the same roof – both often using the same entrance – as in Lorraine; housing livestock and people in independent buildings which are either adjoining, as in Picardy, or dispersed, as in Normandy; or constructing living quarters above the animal quarters, as in Quercy. The peasant was also concerned to have his tools, sheaves of corn, hay and forage crops to hand, for good practical reasons. In areas subject to harsh winters, paticularly the Alps, beasts had to be fed from inside, so hay needed to be near the animals and both had to be easily accessible from the farmhouse, preferably without the necessity of going outside.

Demangeon, among others, identified four basic plan shapes for rural dwellings in France, each of which could include a number of variations: the basic dwelling (*la maison élémentaire*), the compact dwelling (*la maison en ordre serré*), the dispersed dwelling (*la maison en ordre lâche*) and the elevated dwelling (*la maison en hauteur*).

The Basic Dwelling

The basic dwelling placed living quarters and animal quarters side by side under one roof. Because it provided a simple economical dwelling for the poorest peasant, it is to be found scattered all over France with concentrations in certain areas where it became the preferred plan. Both the peasant's family and his beasts were accommodated on the ground floor, with a granary in the roof space for storing food and fodder. This was because the walls were frequently of clay and could not reliably support an upper storey, but the steep pitch required for the thatched roof did give space for a storage loft. Width was sufficient for no more than a single room, again in order to keep the height of the pitched roof and the span and dimensions of roof joists and rafters to a minimum. Extension was consequently along the length. A basic dwelling therefore ranged from a simple two-room cottage, consisting of an all-purpose living room and stable divided by an internal wall or hurdle screen with communicating door, to the 'longhouses' of Brittany and the houses of the Ardennes villages. In these the living quarters, cattle shed, stable, barn, and possibly a lean-to to provide shelter for straw and carts, all formed one long building fronting the street. Behind was a garden, perhaps with a small shed for the pig and in front a dunghill.

In mountainous countryside, particularly in the Auvergne but also stretching westwards into the Limousin and eastwards across the Rhône valley into the Alps, advantage was taken of the steeply sloping ground to place the barn in the upper floor storage area, with access by a short ramp from the upper slope. In areas where cattle must be kept and fed inside over a long winter, this arrangement provided the dry extra storage space needed, gave carts easy access to the barn, allowed cattle to be fed simply by pitching the hay and fodder down in to the mangers and most importantly protected the ground floor against the cold by providing a well-insulated, hay-filled space above.

The most original and developed example of the basic dwelling is to be found in the east of France in Lorraine, Vosges and Franche-Comté. Here one large, almost square-shaped building contained a central barn, flanked on one side by a line of domestic rooms – kitchen, living room and bedroom – and on the other by a line of rooms for the horses, cattle and pigs, all under a single roof. In older houses the only entrance to this building was through the great barn door. Access to the animal quarters on one side and the domestic quarters on the other was via the barn. Above the ground floor a granary occupied the entire loft.

The Compact Dwelling

The compact dwelling consists of a rectangular enclosure, three sides of which, at least, are made up of buildings arranged around a courtyard. The most notable examples of this type of farm building are to be found on the fertile plateaux and plains that cover Picardy and Artois and flow into neighbouring areas of eastern Normandy and Flanders. In these regions it was grain which provided the wealth of the farmers, and this precious commodity was stored in the large barn which occupied a prominent position on the street side next to the entrance leading into the courtyard. Wagons would stop under the eaves of these austere buildings, and sheaths of corn would be tossed through pitch holes in the barn's side. At the end of the working day the carts would all be drawn up by the big doors opening into the courtyard. Opposite these, at the far end of the courtyard, were the living quarters, which were linked to the barn by the stables and the cattle sheds. These formed one side of the courtyard and were usually accessible from the farmer's domestic quarters by internal doors, but otherwise reached by an outside path protected from the elements by a projecting roof. Thus the peasant farmer had easy access to his livestock and could take in the full extent of the yard and surrounding buildings at a glance. This arrangement of human and animal quarters around an internal farmyard was repeated down both sides of a village street, so that one side of a farmer's courtyard was closed by his own stables and cowsheds and the other by the back wall of his neighbour's.

The large isolated farms of the Paris basin use the same compact plan but double it in

Recques-sur-Course
Pas-de-Calais

This farmstead, comprising buildings ranged about a large courtyard, is a good example of the compact dwelling found on the rich soils of the plains of Picardy. The agricultural priorities of the farmstead are shown by the prominence of the symmetrically sited barns which flank the entrance to the courtyard. Wagons would draw up under their eaves so that sheaths of wheat – cut much greener than today and threshed gradually over the winter – could be tossed through the large pitch holes seen here. The imposing, brick-built farmhouse is positioned opposite the courtyard entrance, with wings for the stables and cowsheds completing the enclosure. Flints (*rognons de silex*), found on the clay-covered chalk plateaux of the region, have been used for the barns' foundations, which are retained by stone quoins and may have been the base to earlier timber-framed barns with thatch roofs. These would have been replaced in the nineteenth century by the superstructures seen here, which have pantile roofs and infills of local soft chalk contained within brick quoins, string courses and openings.

a mirror image, so that the imposing entrance to the internal courtyard is flanked by a barn on each side and the courtyard itself has a range of stables and cowsheds down both its sides. The farmhouse still stands opposite the entrance but has grown taller, more imposing, more comfortable-looking. These fortress-like farmsteads, devoted to farming on the grand scale, also stride majestically over Picardy, Artois, Hainault and northwards to Brussels and Limbourg in the Rhineland.

The Dispersed Dwelling

Living on such intimate terms with their beasts did not appeal to everyone and was an arrangement which also had its functional drawbacks. Rather than take livestock from the farmyard to the pasture, it was considered better in some *pays* to bring the pasture to the farmyard. This was the philosophy behind the development of the dispersed farmstead, where the buildings are scattered within an enclosed pasture. Such farmsteads are to be found in the northern coastal countryside of Flanders, Picardy and upper Normandy, where a wet, mild climate encourages grass to grow and allows cattle to stay outside day and night throughout most of the year.

The typical Flemish farm, or *Hofstede*, with its three separate buildings arranged round a small yard containing the dungheap is a local variation of this type. It dominates West Flanders, fades from sight east of Lille, but strengthens southwards down the coast into Boulonnais and coastal Picardy. The colour of these farms of clay and timber provides a contrast to the leaden grey skies of the north. Traditionally the façades are painted in black or yellow, the woodwork of the windows, doors and porches is painted blue and the wall footings are coated with tar.

The type reaches its most extreme and original expression as you enter the Pays de Caux in Normandy. In this area of medium-scale farming around Yvetot and Le Havre, the farm is set within a grass meadow bounded by high earthbanks. The farmhouse is comfortably positioned on the northern boundary to look out across the kitchen garden, the pasture, and the orchard, amidst which are scattered the farm buildings – stable, cowshed, barn, cart-store, sheep pen and bread oven. Within these protective enclaves, with their highly distinctive earthbanks topped by a wind and stock-proof thicket of trees, cows, sheep, hens and horses can wander freely.

The Elevated Dwelling

A common feature of the basic, compact and dispersed dwelling was that the living quarters were located on the ground floor. An inhabited first floor was only found with the better-off peasant and then the main room, the kitchen, still remained downstairs.

Offwiller
Bas-Rhin

A terrace of closed courtyard farms flanks the main street of this village in Alsace. The ground floor of sandstone contains the cowshed, stable, cartshed and toolshed ranged around four sides of a courtyard, which was entered via the large *porte charretière* door for wagons on the right. Further up the street is a small door for pedestrians. The small stone channel protruding through the whitewashed wall discharges waste water onto the street and is part of one large carved stone sink. The upper storey is timber-framed with an infill here probably of rendered sandstone rubble – a construction technique called *colombage*. The flat tiles on the roof with a rounded lower edge are known as *écailles* ('scales') or *queue de castor* ('beaver's tail').

PLANNING THE FARMSTEAD

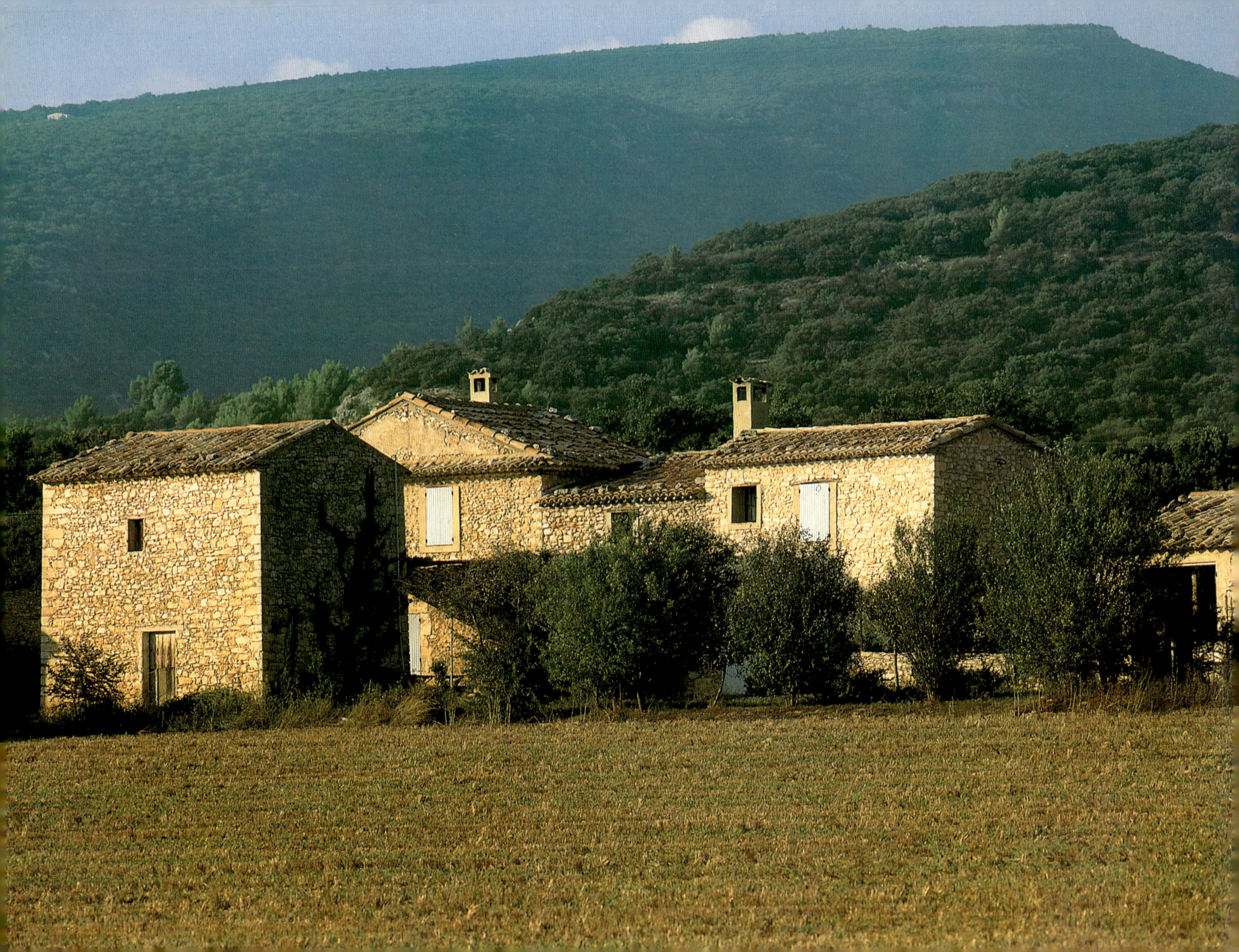

Les Viaux
Vaucluse

Simple geometric forms characterize the Provençal farmhouse. This was because the peasant farmer believed in a form of house which could evolve as needs and means allowed. It started as a simple block or line of buildings and developed to form an L-shape, U-shape or eventually a range of buildings enclosing a courtyard. A shallow single-pitch or double-pitch roof of canal tiles was given to each additional unit. This was built at a height and in a direction best suited to the needs of function and economy, but it gave a visual emphasis to the component parts of a farmstead, creating a massing and overall composition that is one of the most attractive features of the Provençal *mas*, or farmhouse.

But to solve the need to keep a close contact between men, animals and property, a different arrangement evolved, the elevated dwelling, which placed the animals on the ground floor, people on the first and the granary in the roof space. It was self-sufficient, involved few outhouses and included practically everything under the same roof. Curiously it is a plan form rarely found in northern France. It appears under the clearer and sunnier skies of the eastern and southern slopes of the Massif Central, extends onto the plains and hills of parts of the Aquitaine basin and Languedoc and penetrates some way into the Alps.

Placing vertical distance between the farmer and his animals was a trait found not only in southern France but in many Mediterranean areas where good quality surface stone was available to build two-storey farmhouses. In France these elevated houses are scattered about the *départements* of Lot-et-Garonne, Tarn-et-Garonne and Lot. In these limestone buildings with their red tile roofs the cowshed, the cellar or the sheep pens and sometimes an unloading bay were situated on the ground floor. The kitchen and bedrooms were placed on the first floor, access to which was gained by an external staircase leading to a verandah. This open-air gallery, constructed under an overhanging roof, was used as a drying and work area and as a place for the family to gather on summer evenings. Such houses are also found in Languedoc-Roussillon.

The elevated dwelling also became popular with wine-growers on the hills of Beaujolais, Mâconnais and Lyonnais, and it can be found throughout the Massif Central, including the slopes and hills overlooking the Rhône valley, and the chestnut plantations and silkworm country of Cévennes, where farmers supplemented their income by providing the silk trade in Lyon with silk cocoons. In the Ardèche basin the living accommodation on the first floor was reached by an external staircase which led to an enormous covered balcony called the *onlo*. This was really an outside room where you could shelter from the heat of the sun and also hang out cheeses to dry in baskets.

The type is to be found in parts of the French Alps, particularly in Savoy, in the mountainous areas of Dauphiné and as far north as southern Jura. It is as if the southern peoples who populated these areas brought their building styles with them. A squat, stone-built ground floor housing the cattle is topped by a galleried, timber superstructure. As often as not this superstructure is set into a south-facing slope so that immediate access can be gained from the rear into a first floor half-store, while the living accommodation is positioned in front of it behind the south-facing gallery. But this was a place for summer living only. In winter the severity of the climate would force the peasant and his family to descend to the cowshed and share the warmth of the cattle and the insulation of its thick, stone walls.

INTRODUCTION

Building with what lay to hand

To give three-dimensional form to his preferred plan the peasant looked about him for suitable materials. Roads were bad and transport was rudimentary so he would not look far. Nor, as he did not have much to barter with, and certainly no cash, would he seek to buy quarried or manufactured products, especially if they needed to be carried any distance. And of course what was to hand would temper and constrain the plan. Of the materials that were cheap and available he would give preference to those that were durable, weather resistant, load bearing and easy to use. To the French peasant these were the trees in the forest, the reeds in the marsh, the straw from the fields, the gorse and heather from the moors, the stones lying on or just under the surface of the soil and the soil itself.

Clay

Vitruvius, the Roman writer on architecture, when travelling with Julius Caesar on his conquests of Gaul, noted that the Gallic houses were built of mud. Had he made a return trip nineteen centuries later he would have said much the same thing. The Englishman Stothard, travelling in the nineteenth century, remarked that the 'Bretons dwell in huts, generally built of mud'. This sounds primitive, but in fact mud – not the friable topsoil but the clay subsoil – was a good and versatile building material. Walling of clay, called 'cob' in England where it is still commonly found in counties like Dorset and Devon, is known generally as *terre* in France and more particularly as *torchis* or *pisé*. *Torchis* contains additives such as chopped straw and fine gravel whereas *pisé* does not.

Torchis was prepared in the hole from which it was dug, and the hole afterwards would become the farm pond. Water was added to the clay, and the mixture was puddled for several hours. In the Brière region of Brittany until the 1940s puddling was done by men who linked arms to tread the clay barefoot, dancing and chanting as they did so. Then gravel was added to stabilize the material, short lengths of straw to bind it and often cow dung to make it more adhesive. After this the dance was repeated and the resulting *torchis* was left to dry for several days before use. These walls set very hard and provided they were protected from the rain would last for centuries. Protection was provided by large overhanging roofs – which survived as a local building style even when stone and brick had made them unnecessary – and by a coat of tar or a horizontal cladding of timber boarding for the first metre (3 feet) or so above ground level. But the most common form of protection was a rendering of *pisé* – pure liquid clay – which was

Bécherel
Ille-et-Vilaine

Clay-built houses were extremely common in northern France and still exist in this part of Brittany today. They were built from puddled clay *torchis*, which was left to dry for several days before being forked into the walls in 'lifts', or sections, 600–800 mm (2 ft–2 ft 8 in) high. Up to a month was needed between lifts, and the whole building took about six months to construct. The horizontal lines of the lifts can be clearly seen in this example. If the *torchis* was relatively liquid, timber shutters were used, otherwise the clay was simply heaped on the preceding 'lift' and the edges parred with a fork. Foundations were rarely more than 500 mm (1 ft 8 in) deep, if used at all, with a base of stone (seen on the right) wherever possible. Windows and doors were cut out afterwards under timber lintels built into the walls as they went up. This example now has a roof of slate but would originally have been given a cover of wheat or rye thatch, projecting well beyond the eaves to protect the walls.

then limewashed. Visitors who return to Brittany often remember how sharply white and clean the Breton cottages of their youth were, in contrast to their present shabby greyness. This is not an illusion, due to failing eyesight or the nostalgic images of remembered youth, for in the years of *pisé* rendering it was imperative to whitewash your walls every year or so, whereas the painted cement renderings of today's walls can be left to fade with impunity.

Thatch

Almost without exception houses with clay walls were roofed in thatch; indeed in 1728 a traveller in Picardy noted that even the churches were thatched. The predominance of thatch lasted until the industrial revolution of the nineteenth century, when the advent of the railways brought mass-produced rectangular clay tiles to rural France.

Thatch roofs could be of wheat or rye straw, reed, heather or broom according to what lay to hand. The straw, which needed to be at least 1.2 metres (4 feet) long – a great deal longer than the varieties we know today – was cut green, combed to extract the grain, which would otherwise have attracted birds into the roof, and sorted into bundles. These bundles were laid on the roof from the bottom up, and tied to cross poles of ash, chestnut or willow using long split strands of bramble (after the thorns had been removed), rye or willow. Reed, laid in the same way, was used on buildings near to marshes and river estuaries, while heather and broom predominated in upland areas such as the Massif Central. The roof carpentry here was simple: there were no rafters, trusses or purlins, only horizontal poles laid close together with branches of chestnut close woven vertically between them. Into this mesh were pushed handfuls of freshly cut broom or heather, stalks first, to form a roof covering which would last a century in any climate.

Wood

Although forest once covered most of France, the cutting and burning of it to clear the land and the use of wood over the centuries for fuel, shipbuilding, smelting and charcoal-burning gradually led to its loss and decline. This process was accelerated by the peasant's right to graze his pigs, cattle, sheep and goats in the forest, which put a stop to natural regeneration. A further right jealously guarded by the peasant allowed him to take wood for building purposes, until edicts in the seventeenth and eighteenth centuries outlawed the practice in the interests of preserving the few forests remaining.

Trees for building were felled in late autumn and winter on the day after a full moon (which affected sap levels) and were left on site for several months before being

Fraisse-sur-Agout
Hérault

The Prat Alaric farmstead, of which this building is part, lies in the Monts de l'Espinouse, a place of torrential streams and steep rocks covered with the prickly *maquis* ('scrub') from which the *espinouse* ('prickly') name comes, at the south-west extremity of the Massif Central in Languedoc-Roussillon. It is an area of granite, gneiss and mica schist, a fact reflected in the construction of this 38 m (125 ft)-long *pailler*, an upper-level 'straw store' with a south-sloping floor, built in the 1830s. Cattle and sheep are housed on the ground floor. The roof is thatched in two- or three-year-old broom at a steep 60° pitch, using the short, dense purgative broom (*Cytisus purgens*) known locally as *reguers*. It is cut between the time of the first frosts and before the rising of the sap and laid in damp weather, while still fresh, on a light roof structure of beech poles. The ridge is covered by turfs of grass, which have long hairy roots known in the dialect as *pel de can* ('dog's hair') when dug up from the old meadows. The turfs are laid with the dog's hair uppermost.

transported to open drying sheds. This lengthy operation resulted in durable, high-quality wood. Any cutting of the timber was by hand, as steam- (and water-) driven sawmills were a late development. There was therefore a tendency to use timber as found where at all possible. When trees had to be divided, this was done by splitting with wedges and axes, which produced some curious shapes. However the French peasant did not have the same concern for straight edges and right-angles as we do: strangely curved pieces of timber could always be found a place in roofing trusses and timber-framed façades.

Today timber-framed buildings are found in those areas of France where forests have survived: Picardy in the north, Argonne, Champagne and Alsace in the east; Normandy, Maine and Anjou in the west; Sologne and Berry in the centre. These timber-framed buildings had the advantages of speed and simplicity of construction. They could be prefabricated, put together flat on the ground and then lifted into position. The builders of these houses had benefited from skills and techniques developed by shipbuilders and, once constructed, the buildings could be easily dismantled and used again when the owner wanted to move or enlarge his house. Over the centuries, as builders became more inventive in their designs, timber-framed buildings became more and more elaborate, reaching a peak of perfection in Normandy and Alsace.

In the Alps, people drew upon the great conifer forests to construct their houses using larch or spruce poles cut and stacked horizontally one upon the other to form the walls of the house. Larch and spruce were also used to make wooden roof tiles generally known as *bardeaux*. As with thatch, timber tiles were once more prevalent than they are today, being found wherever the forests existed to provide the wood for them; as well as larch, spruce, pine, chestnut, and more rarely oak or beech were used. These timber shingles always had to be split along the length of the grain if they were to last. Traditionally they were split from trees that were selected from the shaded side of the mountain, where slower growth produces a finer grain, and felled during the last moon of November on a day free of frost. They were either nailed to cross battens or, where the pitch was shallow, simply laid on the roof and held down with stones and logs. Longer planks, 2–3 metres (7–10 feet) long, were laid two-deep on steeper pitches; shorter planks, some 450 millimetres (1 foot 6 inches) long, were laid three-deep on shallow pitches, and sometimes even five-deep in the Jura. Wood tiles provide a roof covering which gives good insulation, keeps the snow on the roof, and if well maintained will last a century, longer if turned. Their great disadvantage, as with thatch, is their susceptibility to fire.

Nancray
Doubs

Originally built in 1770, this farmhouse in the Écomusée of Nancray in Franche-Comté is typical of the Sundgau region of southern Haut-Rhin in Alsace. Although the Sundgau is situated on the borders of both Switzerland and Franche-Comté, the architectural influences in this land of lakes and woods come from the Alsatian plain. The vernacular architecture is nevertheless distinctive and rustic in a countryside more human and rural than the rest of Alsace. The roofs form a broad canopy with a pronounced hip, wide gable and a steep pitch. The timber framework tends to be simple and uncomplicated with the few diagonal braces running through a number of horizontal members. The infill is made with yellow sand from the nearby Jura and often has a border in white, as here, to emphasize the geometrical composition of the timber work. Called *scraffito*, this decoration is produced by cutting an edge into the lime mortar render while it is still wet and then highlighting it with whitewash. Inside, a broad fireplace discharges its smoke into the roof space, so there is no chimney piece to be seen externally.

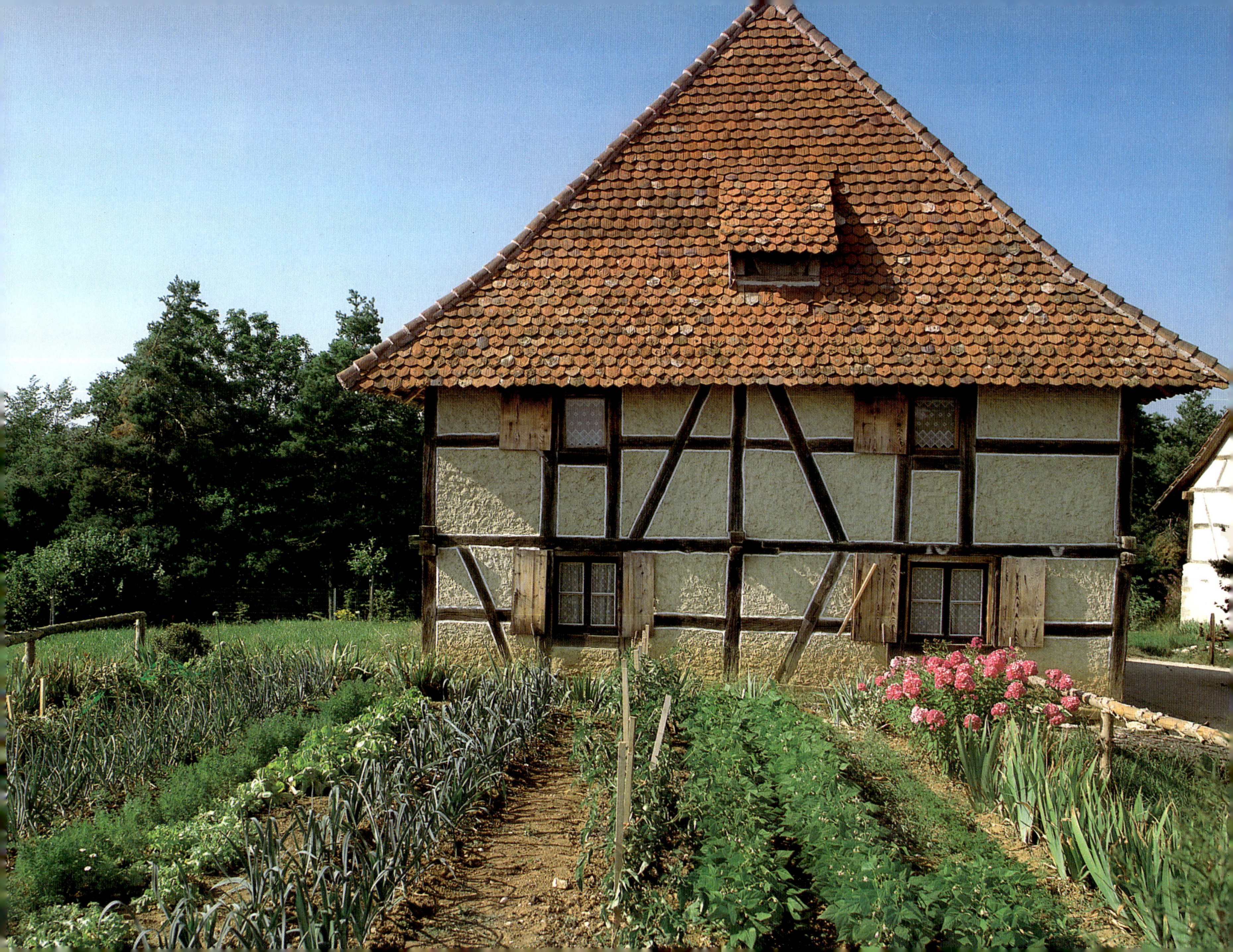

Field stone

Stone was the preferred building material, but it had to be easily available locally and of good quality. In northern and central France, with the exceptions of the extreme eastern and western edges, it was not. The chalk found locally was mostly of poor quality, and where it was used, as in the Loire valley, it weathered badly and had to be supported by better, more expensive stone at the quoins and openings. Central, northern France was consequently a country of earth structures – *torchis* and *pisé* – until the nineteenth century when cheap brick could be produced locally from rich deposits of clay. One of the best building stones used in the north was flint from the clay-covered chalk plateaux. Although difficult to work, it was knapped – cut in half in order to provide two flatter surfaces – and again used between quoins and window and door surrounds of wood, stone or brick. Although knapped-flint work was never used as extensively in northern France as it was in the eastern counties of England, the dense, impervious qualities of flint were useful in these wet northern lands for providing foundation courses to buildings. Constructions of *torchis* and timber, often replaced by brick in the nineteenth century, could be placed on these comparatively water-resistant footings.

South of the Loire, however, France is largely and abundantly a land of stone. In the swathe of limestone and sandstone country wrapped round the granite and schist outcrops of the Massif Central, the Alps and Pyrenees, good-quality building stone runs through the thin soils. There was never any shortage as ploughing and the action of running water and winter frosts would constantly bring good, hand-sized fragments of rock to the surface, which would regularly be cleared by the women and children of the villages and heaped in piles. There, exposed to the air, and to heat and rain and frost as season followed season, the worst would deteriorate whilst the best would set firm and hard. The better stones were then sorted according to their potential use; large blocks for keystones, voussoirs, lintels and quoins; slabs for roofs and floor tiles; and small hand-sized squares and rectangles for walls.

Elsewhere, debris resulting from erosion and glacial action on mountain outcrops also provided readily available building materials. Everywhere great rivers chipped, rounded and rolled stones along their courses to the point where local builders could pick them up for use in their houses. This created highly distinctive styles of architecture, as in the Rhône valley where river-rounded stones were laid diagonally in a fishbone pattern, *en arête de poisson*, which probably has its origins in Roman building techniques. Where stone was naturally stratified or could be fashioned to provide flat surfaces, dry-stone walling was common. Slates, schists, shales, mudstones and sedimentary rocks such as limestone and sandstone could be used in this way. Indeed, such dry-stone techniques could also be employed to make the roofs too, as in the beehive-shaped shelters to be seen in Périgord, Provence, the Haute Loire and Burgundy.

Dressed stone

Dressed stone was a rich man's building material, because it had to be quarried and cut, and good stone quarries were few and far between. They were commercial enterprises, employing a work force whose wages had to be met by the cost of the stone. In these noisy centres of activity, marked by a slowly rising pall of dust in an otherwise tranquil countryside, rock was blasted apart in large quarries and then split using wedges. In soft sedimentary rock, iron wedges were driven into the lines of stratification with the precision of a jeweller cutting a diamond. Hard, igneous stones were split by wooden wedges, which were soaked repeatedly until their expansion cracked the stone apart, like a knife twisting in the joint of a walnut shell. Quarried stone was difficult to transport because it was so heavy. Dressed-stone or ashlar buildings required a team of professional masons: a further disincentive to the peasant. On the other hand, once it was up, a stone building would last, and the dressed stone could be used over and over again as building replaced building. One consequence of this was that door and window openings remained the same size for centuries, so that the expensively quarried and transported cut stones which made up their frames could be used repeatedly.

The most rewarding stone to work with was sedimentary rock, whether the deep-red sandstones of the northern Vosges or the soft, ochre limestones of the Dordogne, for they could be cut with a saw, split and shaped, carved and decorated. The igneous rocks to be found in Brittany, the Cotentin peninsula, the Auvergne and the Cévennes are by contrast difficult to work and shape. The result was that stone in sedimentary areas could be shaped to suit the building whereas in igneous areas buildings had to suit the stone. On the other hand, the resistance of these granites and basalts to harsh conditions (conditions in which they are naturally found) and the skill with which walls were constructed from them are remarkable.

Stone tiles

Slate (*ardoise*) can be split into thin, light, waterproof slices which make a first-class roofing material. It was used where it was found, in Normandy, the Ardennes and the Pyrenees, but the purest and best came from Brittany (slates from the Pyrenees, for example, could be disfigured by veins of iron, which tended to expand and split).

INTRODUCTION

Dagny-Lambercy
Aisne

The monumental *porche-pigeonnier* – combined porch and dovecot – in this picture is typical of the Thiérache region in Picardy found on the western flank of the Ardennes and north of the great plains of the Aisne. It is a pastoral countryside of hedges and quietly grazing cows. The milk is used to make the Maroilles cheese named after the monastery of the same name, where the cheese was first made in the tenth century. Large courtyard farms like this one cluster about the village church, which, in what until the seventeenth century was a frequently invaded frontier country, served as a fortified refuge equipped with a bread oven and a well. The walls of this farmstead are constructed in Flemish bond brickwork, but the big overhangs and hips of the grey-blue, Ardennes-slate roofs, the characteristic, *nez cassé* ('broken nose') effect of the porch gable and the ornate vertical slate cladding perpetuate a design originally conceived to protect walls of clay and wood. The delightful weathervane (*girouette*) elegantly completes the cupola of the *porche-pigeonnier*.

Although Brittany slates had long been exported by sea around the world, it was only with the development of better transport and roads in the nineteenth century that slates reached the rest of northern France, where steeply pitched roofs of thatch and timber shingle could easily be re-covered with superior and fireproof slates. As slates require a steep pitch in order to throw off rain, they have never been a suitable replacement for the clay canal tiles on the shallow pitched roofs of southern France.

Schists, sandstone and especially limestone were also quarried locally to provide stone roof tiles, commonly called *lauzes* or *laves*. Removal of the top soil revealed a crust of stone in large layered slabs, thick and extremely heavy. At a time when nails were forged individually and it was in any case difficult to drill through stone, these tiles were laid at a shallow pitch so that they would be anchored by their own weight. In areas where wood was plentiful, as in parts of the Alps, the timber roof structure could be designed to take the load; high winds and the need to keep snow on the roof anyway made shallow pitches preferable. In areas where timber was scarce, the weight of the tiles had to be carried to the external stone walls. In Quercy and on the limestone *causses* of the Cévennes, for example, limestone vaults carried the weight of the *lauzes* to the outside wall. Alternatively very steep roofs with a light timber framework allowed the limestone slabs to be laid horizontally one upon the other, but with each tile very slightly set in from the one below, as can be seen in the beehive roofs of Provence and the Dordogne.

Clay tiles

Much more popular in the great sweeps of limestone and sandstone country of the south were the clay canal tiles introduced by the Romans: the *tuile romaine* is still to be found in the Midi, and particularly in Provence, Rome's first 'province' in Gaul. There are two elements: the under-tile – a flat, trapezoidal piece of clay made into a canal by turning its edges up; and the over-tile – a half-round trapezoidal piece of clay, giving a wider diameter at one end than at the other. Lapped one over the other and with rain-water running off the convex over-tile into the under-tile, they created a most efficient roof covering which could accommodate the shallow pitches and sudden downpours of the south. Because the Roman system required two shapes of tile to make a roof, a more flexible system, in which the half-round upper tile (the *tuile ronde*, or canal tile) was also used underneath the other way up in order to form a water channel, crossed into southern France from Spain in the eleventh century and gradually overtook the Roman system in popularity. In the north of France, in Picardy and Flanders, a similar tile called the *panne flamande*, or pantile, combined the over-and-under, ridge and furrow shape of the *tuile ronde* system, introduced there by the Spanish in the sixteenth century, into one 'S'-shaped tile.

In eastern France the steep roofs which the Cistercian monks wanted to put on their Burgundian monasteries in the eleventh century would not allow the use of the *tuile ronde*. They therefore created a small, flat tile, or *tuile plate*. Originally known as the *tuile de Bourgogne*, it gradually replaced the fire-prone thatch and timber shingles prevalent in the rural buildings of northern France. By the middle of the nineteenth century these tiles were being mass-produced comparatively cheaply and had come into general use. In central France unadorned, flat, rectangular clay tiles predominated, but a more ornate version with a rounded lower edge like fishscales or beaver tails, *tuiles en queue de castor* – designed to steer rainwater away from the joint between the tiles – developed in the east, in Alsace and Franche-Comté.

Bricks

The conversion of France to fired clay building products did not stop at tiles. Clay bricks baked in the sun had long been used in the south – in Aquitaine for example – in walls that could be sheltered from the rain. Fired clay bricks later gradually percolated through France, entering Languedoc and Aquitaine in the thirteenth century and the Loire valley in the fifteenth, but their production in open-air kilns, fuelled initially with wood and then with charcoal, was expensive. Cheap, mass-produced bricks did not become available until 1860 with the development of the continuously fired furnace. Then northern France saw teams of Belgian brickmakers moving into Flanders and Picardy, bringing their knowledge and setting up brickworks where suitable clay was to be found. Thus from 1860 onwards a countryside whose thatched buildings had formerly melted into the landscape gradually became dotted with prominent red buildings.

Siting for gods, climate and geography

Decisions on siting and orientation were governed entirely by practical considerations, by the need to protect plant, animal and human life in ways which made the least demands on the resources available, in terms of both manpower and materials. The need for water, warmth, shelter, shade, ease of access to the best land, and a healthy growing environment for men and beasts was therefore paramount. In the lowlands you avoided marshland; in the uplands you avoided the dank cold mists of the valley bottoms. In the high Alpine valleys you placed your house on the sunny side of the valley, at the meeting point between the lower meadowland and the high summer pasture.

From Picardy to Provence you wrapped your courtyard farms about the well. In the dry limestones of the Jura and the Cévennes you looked to your roof for your water supply: snow in winter, rain in summer, channelled by timber gutters into clay-lined cisterns. But as life was so precarious and unpredictable, you also chose your site to suit the gods, pagan and Christian. Extreme care was taken to avoid sites that might prove to be unlucky. In Morbihan in Brittany two chickens were buried in their plumage in the middle of the proposed building site, and if after a number of days they were still found to be intact it was considered that the spirits had refused the offering, thus showing their displeasure in the choice of site. Breton masons also believed that if the chosen site was not sprinkled with the blood of a cock, the first person to enter the house would die within the year, for once the threshold of the door had been put in place, Ankou, the personification of death, would seat himself upon it to wait for the first occupant. Only the sacrifice of an animal, or sometimes the burial of an egg beneath the hearthstone, would appease him.

The siting of a building and its orientation were influenced principally by two natural forces: the prevailing wind, which could bring destruction, and the sun, which brought life. The peasant sought to close his building to strong winds, and open it up to gentle sun. As his farmhouse would be built to last many lifetimes, he chose his site with care, taking a year to study it in all seasons and all weathers. He would notice the direction of the soft summer breezes and the worst winter storms, measure the value of every tree and contour, mark the frost hollows, track the path of shadows, and record the effects of land form on the rising and setting sun. Knowing all this could make the difference between enjoying natural air-conditioning and suffering intolerable heat, thus helping to produce a building that would be cool in summer, warm in winter and dry and healthy all year round.

The very word 'orientation' derives from the orient, the east, which has always been the most important point on the compass, associated with the coming of a new day, new hope, new life. Cool and refreshing, the morning sun is delightful even in the hottest climates, and frequently farm buildings and whole villages are orientated towards the south-east in order to benefit from this precious morning light. Turning towards the south helps to pick up the winter sun and track the summer sun for longer through the sky. The value of the sun differs from season to season: in winter the

Saint-Cassien
Dordogne

This cleverly sited farmstead (in Aquitaine) is notched by means of cut and fill into the side of a south-facing hill. The henhouse, woodshed and pigsty on the left are built against a retaining wall surmounted by a shelter belt of trees, which together protect the farmstead from the cold winds of the north. To the right the combined kitchen and living room is set in this sheltered lee but opens to the west and east. It is protected from the heat of the summer sun by the enveloping bulk of an adjoining barn and cowshed on its southern flank to the right. Combined with its thick limestone walls, this makes it a room which is warm in winter and cool in summer. Beyond is a wing of east-facing bedrooms with a *cave* under the southern end. A tall elm on the right, one of the few so far to have survived Dutch Elm disease, provides a shady sitting-out area by the front door. It was once struck by lightning which possibly changed its chemistry and made it unattractive to the beetle that carries this fungus.

noonday sun dips to the south and penetrates the house, where its diminished strength is welcome; in summer the southern sun is terrifying in its strength at noon, but an overhang or a vine-covered arbour will provide welcome shade.

A west-facing position is far and away the worst in summer, when the declining sun is penetrating and supercharged with heat rays of the red and infra-red range. The west and the north are the worst orientations for fruit trees and vineyards which is why all French vineyards are planted on the south-east or east side of a hill.

The north means a cold, sunless aspect, and it is also the direction from which the icy winds of the mistral come tearing down the Rhône valley. Along the course of the Rhône and into Provence and the Camargue, farm buildings turn their backs on the mistral. In the Camargue the simple whitewashed *cabanes* with their reed-thatch roofs have a half-round, apse-like end pointing directly north to help this vicious wind on its way. In the Lubéron region of Provence the stone-built farms show little of themselves to the north, being either cut into or built onto a south-facing slope or hillside. Rarely will a window be cut into the north façade to offer a point of weakness to the wind. Further north, beside the higher reaches of the Rhône, on the high plains of the Ardêche and into Burgundy, the tiled roofs sweep low to the ground on the northern façade offering an aerodynamic shape to the advancing wind. In the Jura half-hipped roofs, called *croupettes*, on the gable ends of the farm buildings help the wind over the roof, and the ridge always points into the prevailing wind in order to ensure that the wind is not heaping snow against the roof.

The Normans, a seafaring and compass-conscious race, built their farmhouses with steep roofs like the hulls of ships and anchored them upside-down on the land. On the western, windward end they constructed a hip-roof shaped like a ship's bow, while the eastern, sheltered end was kept open like the stern galley of an eighteenth-century man-of-war, with a flight of steps – perhaps protected by a projecting half-hip – leading up to the loft. The single chimney sat astride the ridge at the western end, where it could draw at the slightest breeze.

Once the site had been chosen, the plan laid out, the materials chosen and the farmstead built, there were still a few formalities to observe before the peasant, his family and his livestock could move in. No one would enter a newly built house unless preceded by a domestic animal, a dog, cat or hen. Then the parish priest would bless the inside of the house by sprinkling holy water on the floor, and a portion of this dampened floor would be dug up and kept in a small bag as a talisman against illness.

A cross would be placed on the ridge of the roof, carved into a lintel, or painted on a wall. A bouquet would also be placed on the ridge, and a celebratory meal given to family, friends and the masons, carpenters, tilers or thatchers who had helped with the construction of the house. Indeed the builders were usually fed throughout the work in part-payment, and in the Morbihan area of Brittany the thatcher would set flower seeds in the clay cappng of the roof if he had been well fed. If the food had left something to be desired, on the other hand, the owner would find weeds in his ridge capping.

Taking the past into the future

What is extraordinary is that this peasant economy, locked into *pays* buried deep in the French countryside survived intact until the unprecedented prosperity of the thirty years from 1945 to 1975. In 1945, 35 per cent of the French population lived directly off the land; today only 8 per cent do so. In those thirty years the peasant communities of rural France changed more than they had changed in the previous three hundred years, as France switched from an agriculture-based to an industry-based economy. But the farm buildings which embody that long peasant tradition are still there: picturesque anachronisms or potent images of the past. Increasingly they are being viewed as essential bridges between the past and the future. These buildings, so magnificently designed to fit their environmental niche, so imbued with a sense of place and a sense of belonging, can carry the values of the past into the future, to be exploited by generations to come. The children of those peasants who left the land in their millions after the last war to find a new life in the towns and cities are returning to find their roots in the countryside. One French family in nine has a second home in the countryside. Two million farmhouses and cottages are used in this way: a world record. Only one family in fifteen has a second home in the United States, one in one hundred and forty in Germany, one in two hundred in Britain.

Better transport, communications and technology are now enabling more people to find work in or from the villages of France. With agriculture in decline diversification in French farming is as important today as it was in the past, and now offers more scope and opportunity for rural employment. Tourism has brought a market for traditional local goods, more jobs and an appreciation of the rich vernacular heritage of France. The present population of rural France, some 22 million, is much the same as it was at the end of the eighteenth century. Indeed, the composition of the countryside remains the same, with territories still divided into *pays* and related to small *bourgs*. A shift in population between agricultural village and *bourg* may have occurred, but the villages are still on the same sites, still working their land. If anything they are in better heart, with tractors replacing the former teams of horses, greater breadth to their economic base and a more caring attitude to their built inheritance.

The richness, variety and diversity of that inheritance is there to be seen and enjoyed. The farmhouses and cottages in this book (which, it should be noted, have been identified in the caption titles by the name of their village or the village closest to them, together with the *département*) can only hope to give a tantalizing glimpse of what France still has to offer in such abundance. A slightly different itinerary would have brought in other *pays* with rural buildings just as earthy or ethereal, just as solid or light, just as beautiful and just as ingenuous as these. But hopefully there is enough here to inspire a curiosity to explore the vernacular tradition of France – a tradition whose attractions are hard to resist.

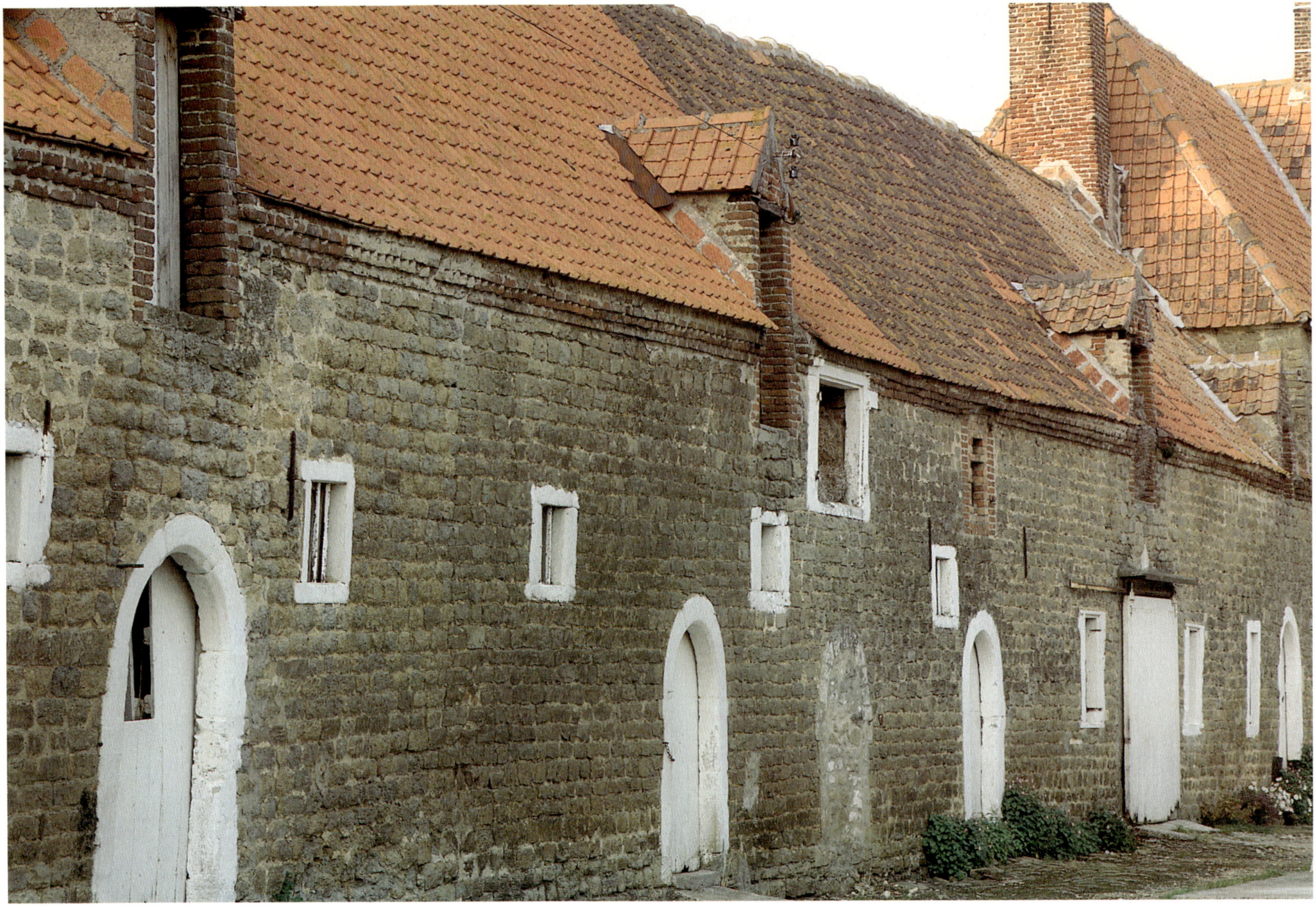

Hesdin l'Abbé
Pas-de-Calais

This stable block, with a series of round-headed entrances, forms part of the courtyard of a large farmstead, which was built of Caen stone (limestone) in 1663. Whereas in Britain the stable door divides horizontally so that top and bottom can open separately or together, in France it is often only the top quarter of the stable door (as here) which opens separately from the rest. Brick has been used to form a corbelled cornice carrying the eaves of the pantile roof and also to provide the frame to the dormers, which give access to the upper floor *grenier*, or loft.

Hesdin l'Abbé
Pas-de-Calais

The courtyard seen opposite also boasts a substantial *pigeonnier*, or dovecot, built of Caen limestone. Until well into the eighteenth century pigeons were the main source of fresh meat in winter because of the need to slaughter most livestock in November, apart from those kept for breeding and working, due to lack of winter fodder. Each brace of birds, which pair for life, will raise a brood of two chicks as frequently as ten times a year for about seven years. Pigeon eggs, which are seldom eaten because the chicks are so valuable, hatch in seventeen days, and the chicks are then fattened by both parents with 'pigeon milk', a secretion resembling a mammalian function unique in the world of birds. At three to four weeks the young birds are tender, juicy, fat and ready for eating without any of the toughness later brought on by flying. They were the original fast food since they could be culled and cooked in twenty minutes. In the seventeenth century there were an estimated 42,000 dovecots in France. This was almost twice as many as in England at the time.

Le Wast
Pas-de-Calais

A subtle range of colours distinguishes the traditional hand-made pantiles on the roof of this terrace cottage facing onto the village green. Its walls are painted white, as at one time were the walls of practically all buildings, from the grandest to the humblest, in order to protect them from the elements. Whitewash was favoured because it was easy to make and its ingredients, chalk dust or lime, available in most areas. A binding material, usually skimmed milk or tallow, was added to this base to help make the whitewash water-resistant and adhesive. Fresh coats of whitewash needed to be applied every year or two although in time a good thick layer of protective lime did build up. If colour was looked for under these grey northern skies, then a range of additives from bull's blood to verdigris, the green discolouring of copper, could be mixed into the whitewash.

Crandal
Pas-de-Calais

The functional use of colour creates a beautiful effect in this farm building in the Boulonnais. Limewash shields the upper part of the *torchis* walls while black pitch on the horizontal boarding protects the lower wall. Thick coats of battleship-grey paint cover the doors and the row of pigeon nesting boxes slung under the eaves of the pantile roof. Rich orange pantiles on the cantilevered dormer roofs protect the openings to the hay loft while a fine cockerel and his six attendant hens add a splash of colour at ground level. If the neighbours wanted a splendid cockerel like this one, they would ask for some of the hens' eggs and place them under their own broody hen. They would choose long eggs, since it was believed that these produced the cocks while the round eggs produced the hens. After twenty-one days the chicks will emerge and a month after that the comb grows on the male chicks, showing whether the right choice had been made.

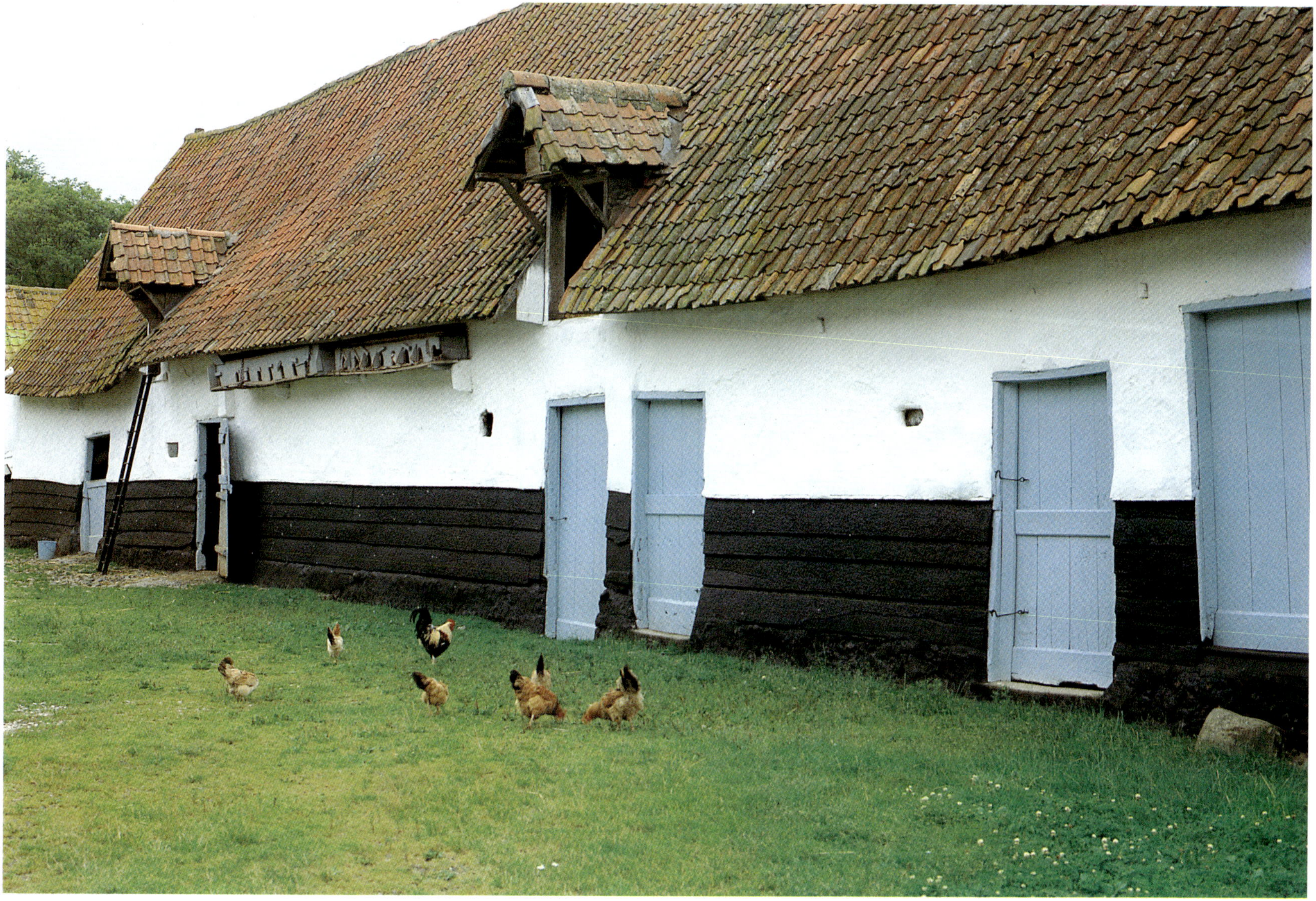

NORD/PAS-DE-CALAIS

Doudeauville
Pas-de-Calais

This seventeenth-century defensive manor farm, seen across its hedged kitchen gardens, is situated beside the River Course (marked by the line of the pollarded willows) on the southern edge of the Boulonnais area of the Regional Park of Nord/Pas-de-Calais. This type of construction – in an area at the edge of France which was fought over by the Spanish, the English and the Burgundians – was characteristic of an aristocracy who were half-warriors, half-farmers. The farmhouse and tower *pigeonnier* are brick-built, but the house has a pantile (*panne flamande*) roof, while the tower has a roof of flat tiles (*tuiles plates*) rising from an ornate brick cornice repeated lower down as a string course. The flight holes in a circle just under the eaves have been simply created by the regular removal of bricks from out of the header bond brickwork.

Doudeauville
Pas-de-Calais

The manor farm at Doudeauville (seen opposite) faces south-east into a courtyard surrounded by single-storey farmbuildings. The external walls that face outwards are made with a locally quarried stone but the walls facing into the courtyard (seen here) are built of the puddled clay and chopped straw mixture called *torchis* on a low stone foundation. The limewash protects the walls from the rain but more substantial protection is provided by the horizontal boarding and the overhang of the pantile roof. The claret red doors are raised off the ground to keep out the mud and water swilling about the farmyard. To the right, the roof is raised slightly to provide the barn doors with sufficient height to allow the entry of loaded carts.

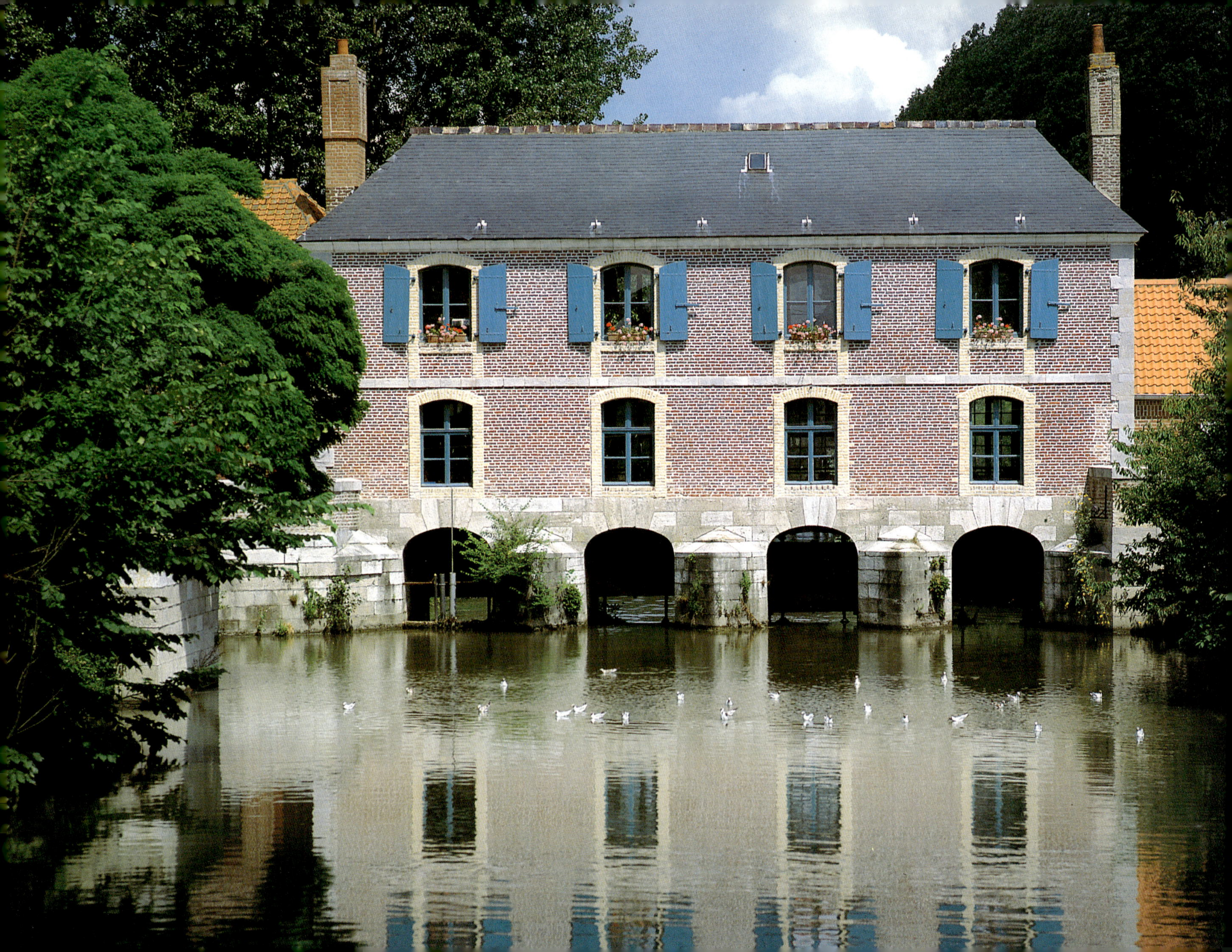

Arques
Pas-de-Calais

The 3,400 hectares (13 square miles) of marshland in the Pas-de-Calais between Flanders and Artois, known as the Marais Audomarois, is a mosaic of waterways and drainage channels controlled by an intricate system of weirs, locks and sluices, created over three centuries. By this means generations of Benedictine and Cistercian monks, together with the local marsh dwellers, have made a habitable and fertile place that is half-water and half-land. Some of the sluices controlling these waters can be seen under this beautifully crafted brick building constructed on a dressed-stone bridge called *Le Grand Vannage* – literally 'The Great Sluice'. It was built as a papermill in the nineteenth century and together with other industrial development in the Saint-Omer region at that period contributed to the pollution of the water of the Audomarois. Today it is a park centre for the Audomarois area of the Nord/Pas-de-Calais Regional Park, whose aim is to conserve the natural beauty, wildlife, traditions and character of the Audomarois, as well as encourage people to enjoy it as a place of recreation.

Saint-Bernard
Pas-de-Calais

The home of the Audomarois marsh dweller, – the 'Maresquiers' or 'Brouckailles' as they were called locally – was a simple affair. It comprised a single living room with an adjoining all-purpose workroom, store and cowshed and possibly a lean-to. Here the cottage is brick built with a pantile roof, but before the nineteenth century the roof would have been covered with reed thatch and the walls clad with horizontal clapboard planks coated with bitumen. The produce of the kitchen garden, a cow and a few other animals, together with fishing and hunting the wild duck that loved these waters, kept the marsh dweller and his family fed on their isolated islands. The cottage faces south onto the waterways which were the only means of reaching neighbours and the outside world until the creation of roads and bridges in the 1970s. Indeed, the post is still delivered and collected along these waterways, with post boxes attached to poles sunk into the water's edge. Flat-bottomed boats made of timber and well-coated in pitch, were used for transport.

Serques
Pas-de-Calais

The railway-crossing keeper's cottage is a familiar sight in the French countryside, having sprung up in the nineteenth century at each point that the new railway system crossed a main road. They were built in the local vernacular style as is this delightful example. Here brick in Flemish bond – alternating headers and stretchers in each row – is used under a roof of the 'mechanical' pantiles that were mass-produced from the end of the nineteenth century in imitation of the original pantile. Brick is also used at the corners of the building in decorative imitation of the time when brick or stone quoins were needed to frame and support walls of clay *torchis* or loose, *tout-venant* stone. These cottages were much sought after as they provided a home, a job and a kitchen garden – *potager* – to tend between trains. Though the home and the garden remain, the job has gone with the coming of automatic railway-crossing gates.

Serques
Pas-de-Calais

The stable wing of this courtyard farm is built of the two materials, brick and pantiles, that came to dominate Picardy and Flanders in the nineteenth century. Before the middle of that century brick was fired in open-air kilns using wood and then charcoal. The process was lengthy and difficult, so the beautiful bricks in subtly varied colours that it produced were too expensive for the common man. However, the invention in 1860 of the continuously fired kiln, using coal which could be more easily transported on the new railways, changed all that. Equally, the pantile – a development of the canal tile introduced by the Spanish in the sixteenth century – could be more readily produced. As a result, what was a countryside of brown and ochre thatch roofs and painted timber or whitewashed clay walls turned red in less than a century.

NORD/PAS-DE-CALAIS

CHAMPAGNE-ARDENNE

Géraudot
Aube

Géraudot sits in the Forêt d'Orient Regional Park, which is an oasis of lakes and forests held between the rivers Seine and Aube. It is part of La Champagne Humide ('Wet Champagne'), an area between Troyes and Saint-Dizier in south-east Champagne where damp, fertile clay soil makes rich pastures and fat cattle. To its north a great and seemingly endless expanse of dry, thin chalky soils with barely a tree to see – La Champagne Sèche ('Dry Champagne') – rolls up to the Ardennes. It is a disconcerting landscape once called La Champagne Pouilleuse (meaning wretchedly poor), where land was sold off *à la hollée* – 'by earshot'. Today artificial fertilizers have turned it into a prosperous wheat plain but its chalk-walled vernacular architecture still reflects the difficult farming conditions of the past. By contrast these timber-framed farmhouses in La Champagne Humide have a wealthy air.

Géraudot
Aube

Timber dominates the construction of this typical farmhouse in the well-wooded Forêt d'Orient Regional Park east of Troyes. An array of close-centred oak uprights, diagonal braces, first-floor joists and rafters structure the building. The infill (*hourdis*) between the timber uprights consists of a ladder of oak pegs set diagonally between the uprights and covered in a mixture of clay, dung and horsehair. A dividing line between the southern use of canal tiles and the northern use of flat clay tiles can be traced through France, running right through this regional park. Géraudot lies north of that line, so flat clay tiles cover this roof, which oversails the eaves to give some protection to the walls.

Lesmont
Aube

La Champagne Humide, in which Lesmont is situated, was rich agriculturally and La Champagne Sêche poor, because of an eastward upfold of the Paris Basin. This enabled the forces of erosion to remove the white chalk, which makes La Champagne Sêche so arid, and expose the fertile clays and sands underneath. This belt of country stretching north-eastwards from Troyes to Vitry-le-François and Bar-le-Duc was covered in forests and swamps. However, a clearing process, begun in the Middle Ages by the great abbeys, created a countryside of meadowlands in the valley bottoms, arable fields up the slopes and orchards on the sheltered, east-facing hillsides. Forests nevertheless remained as an important commercial component of the landscape. Each November woodcutters arrived from the Argonne Massif to work in these forests, leaving in June for the hay-harvest back home. The abundance of wood is reflected in the half-timbered architecture of the La Champagne Humide as can be seen in this farmhouse with its close-centred uprights and flamboyant use of diagonal braces.

Piney
Aube

The construction of this seventeenth-century barn is typical of La Champagne Humide in south-east Champagne. The coursed stone foundations support a timber framework (*pan de bois*) of generously dimensioned, closely placed lengths of oak, which include the occasional diagonal beam among the vertical and horizontals to give added stability. The first floor level, marked by the upper horizontal line of beams on the façade, is placed high to allow carts through the twin cartshed openings, separated by an oak post, and the single opening of the hay and corn barn. The dormer windows (of a type called *lucarne à foin*) have hipped roofs, which are cantilevered well forward in order to hold a pulley system designed to lift sacks of grain and hay bales into the loft for storage. The infill between the timber frame is made up of a puddled clay *torchis* applied over a horizontal lattice of oak battens. The roof, carried well clear of the eaves to protect the walls, is covered with small rectangular clay tiles, ridged canal tiles on the ridge and plain canal tiles on the hip ridges.

CHAMPAGNE-ARDENNE

LORRAINE-VOSGES

Manonville
Meurthe-et-Moselle

On both sides of the broad village streets of Lorraine terraces of identical farmsteads, built to the same plan and specification, present a repeated pattern of openings to the world. The sequence of barn door, cowshed window, cowshed door, farmhouse door, living-room window and kitchen sink window is repeated by each farmstead down the street. These openings are framed by dressed limestone slabs while the rest of the wall is made of limestone rubble, coated with a clay *pisé* render. All these buildings are enclosed under one large shallow-pitched roof of half-round clay tiles, the only substantial area north of the Loire where they are found. The broad street and characteristically wide pavements called *aisances* were treated as a communal farmyard and would have been a riot of carts, wagons, farm implements, dung heaps, wood stores, tethered animals, lines of ducks looking for a way out, foraging hens and strutting cockerels. At the back of the farmsteads peace could be found in walled orchards and kitchen gardens.

Bisping
Moselle

This area on the eastern edge of Lorraine, called the Pays des Etangs, has a vernacular style of architecture which is not typical of either Lorraine or Alsace but marks a transition between the two. The plan and large size are characteristic of Lorraine but the detachment of the farmhouse and its elevational treatment, using a timber framework on a ground floor of masonry construction and a roof covering of flat tiles, are typical of Alsace. In the farmstead terraces of Lorraine, only the end buildings have an exposed gable end. Here each farm has two exposed gable ends, so the west-facing end is often protected from the prevailing winds and rains by a cladding of timber shingles, called *tavaillons*.

Offwiller
Bas-Rhin

This is a fine example of an eighteenth-century farmhouse (now a museum) with barn and dependent buildings on the left. Because it lies at the edge of the beech-covered sandstone outcrops of the Vosges du Nord, the house is a substantial, red sandstone building, even though it would have been lived in by a humble, two-cow, peasant farmer. Away from this sandstone area only wealthy farmers, known as *coqs de village*, could afford to build with sandstone. The external steps lead up to a kitchen and living-room on the first floor, with a small store and two bedrooms on the next floor. The living room, called a *gross stub*, would have an ornate tiled stove, the *kachelofen*, and an alcove, into which the main bed was built. The arched door on the ground floor opens into the *cave*, or 'cellar', where the wine and potatoes are stored and where *eau de vie* ('brandy') was made. Six litres of wine is distilled to make one litre of *eau de vie*. Drink a little too much and it works through your body like some exotic poison; the brain remains perfectly lucid but the body feels completely paralysed.

Offwiller
Bas-Rhin

A roof without chimneys normally indicates a farm building rather than a farmhouse – not so in Alsace. Chimneys were not commonly built into houses until the nineteenth century. Before that, smoke emptied into the roof space and found its way out through the tiles with the help of a through-draught created by these triangular openings at the apex of the gable ends. The only problem was that this could also let in the devil. However, a wrought-iron grille or, better still, a sharp spike would protect the house from such an unwanted visitor. To the peasant of Alsace the devil was everywhere: in the sicknesses of cattle, in bad harvests and in the all-too-frequent fire disasters.

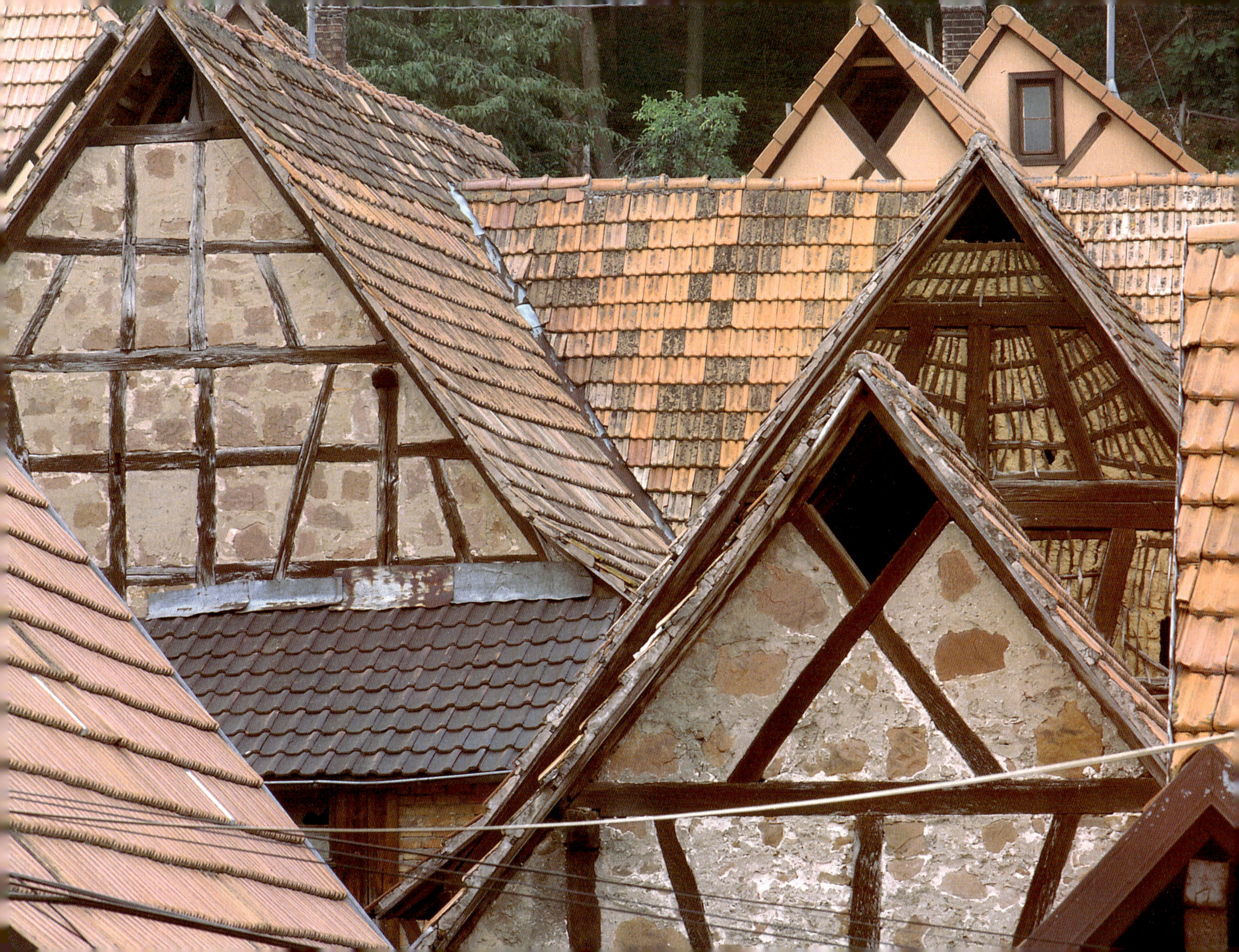

Truchtersheim
Bas-Rhin

A small village dominated by large farmsteads, Truchtersheim is situated in the fertile region of Kochersberg. Once the granary of Strasbourg, the area has a highly distinctive checkerboard landscape with its fields of cereals, tobacco and hops. This closed courtyard farmhouse has been continuously developed since 1826. The thick base of sandstone rising through one and a half floors to allow light into the cellars is an expression of wealth, considering the village's position so far south of the quarries. The timber patterning of the upper storey – the *colombage* – uses a symbolic language, which was not simply functional or decorative. It denoted the wealth, rank and profession of the owners, and was also believed to bring happiness, good luck and to keep away the evil eye. Here the use of symbolic language is restricted to a lozenge barred by the cross of St Andrew while the timber patterns rising the full height of the upper storey are examples of a pagan symbol of German origin, the *Motif du Mann*.

Truchtersheim
Bas-Rhin

The family and servants would live on the eastern side of these internal courtyard farmsteads. The stone external staircase, which rises over the large entrance to the *cave* or cellar, led up to the living accommodation, which included a living room for the *domestiques* and *anciennes alcoves* for the old folk. Above, an open timber gallery has access to the bedrooms. Farmbuildings, including barn, cowshed, cartshed, stable, pigsty, laundry and bread oven, are ranged round the other three sides of the courtyard. Such facilities, together with a walled orchard and kitchen garden against the eastern façade, made these Alsatian farmhouses into near self-sufficient units.

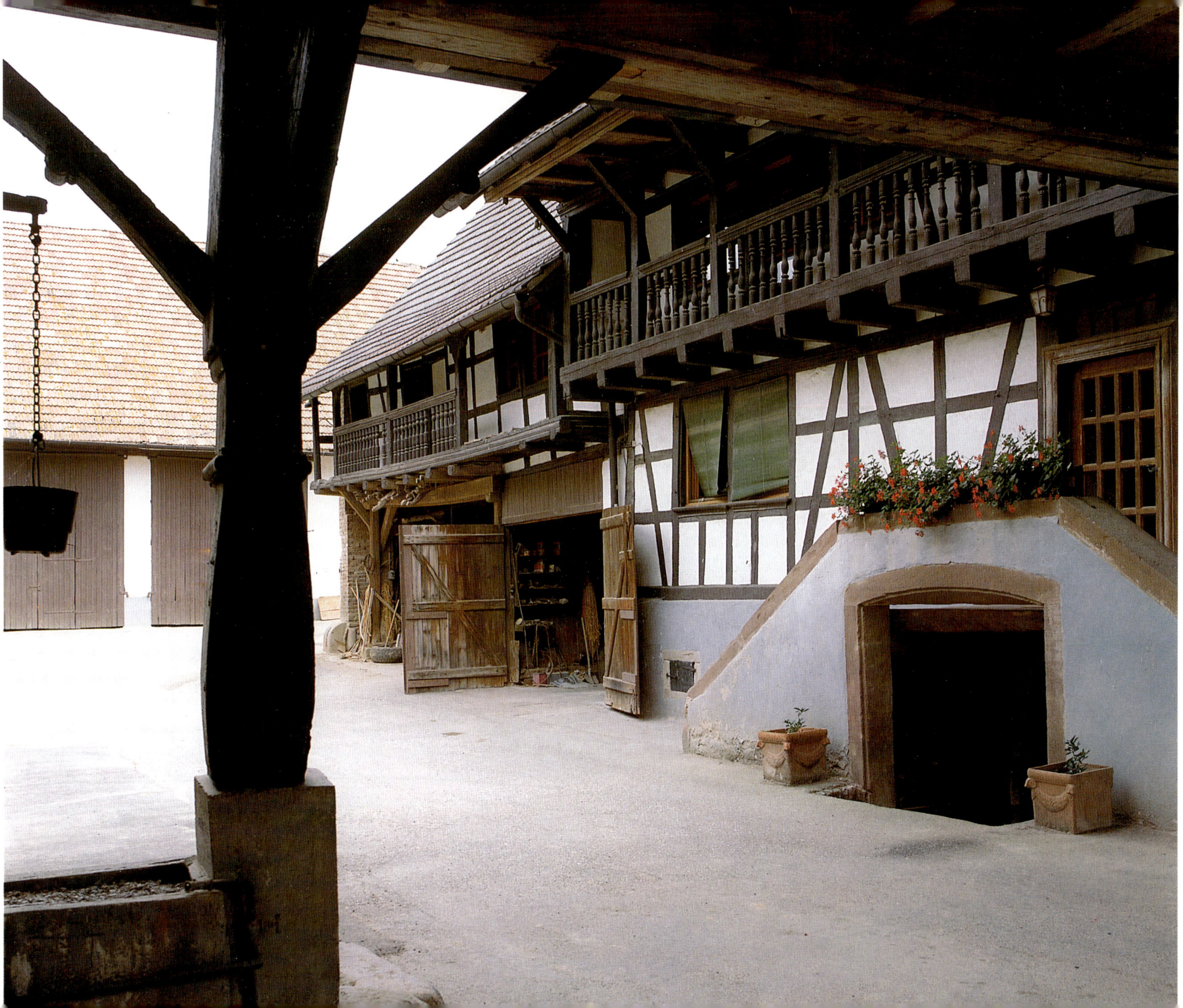

Imbsheim
Bas-Rhin

Imbsheim is a small village with a population of some 600 people at the heart of the ancient *pays* of Hanau, whose capital, Bouxwiller, lies a few kilometres to the north-east. Situated on flat land between two limestone outcrops, the village wraps tightly about the spire of the protestant church, or *temple* (as protestant churches are called in France), at its centre. Mixed farming of cereals, potatoes, sugarbeet, tobacco, stock-rearing and fruit-growing provides its living. Here the sliding door of a *porte charretière* has been slid back to reveal the inner courtyard of a typical village farm. Open timber steps lead up to a projecting half-timbered hay loft, fronted by a beautifully detailed gallery and balustrade. Handmade *tuiles écailles* – flat clay tiles with rounded ends – cover the roof.

Mittelbergheim
Bas-Rhin

This small wine-growing village, on the hills separating the Rhine Valley from the foothills of the Vosges mountains, is officially designated *L'une des plus beaux villages de France*. It is a collection of twenty-one *maisons vigneronnes* – 'winegrowers' houses' – huddled shoulder-to-shoulder about a crossroads. The Caves Boeckel shown here, which make and sells the Vins d'Alsace including Blanc de Blancs, Pinot Noir, Rieslings and, with the grapes that do not ripen, the sparkling Crémant d'Alsace, are situated at the centre of the village. The Boeckel family have been living and working in these buildings since 1573. The red sandstone entrance arch, in the traditional *anse de panier* ('basket handle') shape, provides access to courtyards, under which is a vast basement of interconnecting wine cellars.

Hunspach
Bas-Rhin

Hunspach is a beautiful village, just outside the North Vosges Regional Park and not a stone's throw from the Second World War Maginot Line. Its nineteenth-century houses are uniformly half-timbered and superbly crafted. The detail of this casement window with its lightly curved head provides a delightful example. The curve of the outermost frame flattens at its edges to meet the vertical rail at right angles. Also noteworthy are the well-judged proportions of its glass panels and the thinness of its joinery and glazing bars. The shutters are made of no more than two pieces of wood and close into recesses cut within the window frame so that once shut they cannot be lifted out of their hinges. Owners took a pride in their buildings and liked to sign them as they have so elegantly done here. The name or initials of the owners and the date of construction were often joined by a symbol of their trade or profession, like the *serpe* ('billhook') for the winegrower, the mallet for the cooper, the scissors for the tailor, the bread roll for the baker or the horseshoe for the blacksmith.

Quatzenheim
Bas-Rhin

A small Frenchman came up to me in this ancient village on the Roman road to Strasbourg. It was a warm, spring morning and the village had seemed deserted. 'Can I help you, Monsieur?' he asked. 'Why perhaps you can, Monsieur', I replied. 'I was standing here noting how the vertical furrowing on these beautiful tiles gives such a wonderful texture to the roof in this morning light, but why are they there?' 'Ah,' he said, 'I think I can help you there, since as a child I watched my grandfather at work in the *tuilerie*. You must remember these are handmade tiles. Clay was thrown in a wooden mould and the surplus scraped off. These are the marks of a man's fingers, Monsieur!' We were both delighted with this communication and stood there slapping imaginary clay into imaginary moulds with much animation and laughter. The formerly deserted street became busy with bedroom windows being thrown open, bedding hung out to air and heads craning out to see what all the palaver was about.

ALSACE

Henflingen
Haut-Rhin

In the 1870s the carpenter gave way to the mason as stone and brick replaced the timber-framed buildings for which Alsace had been renowned for centuries. Before that a house was built by the carpenter. He was a much respected professional, a member of a guild which set high standards of craftsmanship and behaviour and controlled the entry into the profession through a rigorous apprenticeship scheme. Dynasties of such carpenters became established in the region: the Schini family, for instance, settled in the Hanau area of northern Alsace in the seventeenth century and left its mark on many farmhouses in the Bouxwiller and Kochersberg region. Before constructing a house, the carpenter would draw the design on a large wooden platform, which was laid out on the village green. He would do this bearing in mind the timber at his disposal, which was mostly oak used 'green', within a year of being felled. A dry assembly of all the timber members for the façades would take place on the platform with each member numbered, before construction began on the actual site.

Riquewihr
Haut-Rhin

Lines of vines rise above the steep pitch of a roof covered in handmade *queue de castor* ('beaver's tail') tiles – a type rarely found outside eastern France. The smaller roof openings (called *houteaux*) are also typically Alsatian and give light and air to the *grenier*. The secret to producing wine so far north lies in the Vosges mountains which, rising high to the west, draw off the moisture from the damp westerly winds and leave an east-facing slope of vines to enjoy the second driest climate in all of France. Goethe, a Rhinelander no distance away in Frankfurt, noted with astonishment the sudden and early inrush of spring in northern Alsace. While autumn storms might rock the rest of France, here, year after year, the imperturbable grape continues to ripen unhurriedly in calm, sun-filled days.

Ensisheim
Haut-Rhin

Glazed clay tiles in reds, greens, yellows and browns, covering church spires and the roofs of châteaux, dovecots, barns and farms, light up the countryside of eastern France in sudden splashes of colour, like this example at Ensisheim Écomusée (buildings museum) near Mulhouse. Curiously, they are little used outside Alsace and Burgundy although they have followed the Saône and Rhône south to wash up on roofs here and there in Provence, often in the more subdued colours of chocolate browns and yellow ochres. White storks (*Ciconia ciconia*), the national bird of Germany, make an even more selective use of France, breeding only in Alsace and Lorraine. The stork is also the national emblem of Alsace, whose people are greatly attached to these migrating birds and were extremely concerned when only three pairs returned to Alsace for the summer of 1981. The reason for this was put down to the draining of marshes and winter-time hunting in Africa. The Alsatians are trying, with some success, to rebuild the population by mating wild birds with storks reared in captivity and by constructing nesting platforms on their buildings.

Ensisheim
Haut-Rhin

This fisherman's house in the Écomusée comes from the Ried, a stoney and swampy area of Alsace bordering the Rhine. It was built with the pebbles and rich clay deposits washed down the river, which were used in two different ways to produce the infill for an economical framework of timber, since trees were scarce. In some parts of the structure doughnut-like rings of puddled clay were threaded onto sticks of hazel and set upright and side by side between the timber posts; in others, horizontal layers of river pebbles sandwiched between layers of fired clay tiles were used as infill. Pebbles were also used as a damp-proof foundation on which to construct the timber frame. The lazy curves to the timber diagonals illustrate how the boughs of trees were used as found and simply split with an axe or adze. Since there was no shortage of marsh reed, the roof was naturally built of thatch, which projects well beyond the eaves to protect the clay and timber walls. Good reed thatch will last for 75–100 years, whereas straw thatch lasts for 25–30 years. Certainly these storks seem to have every confidence in it.

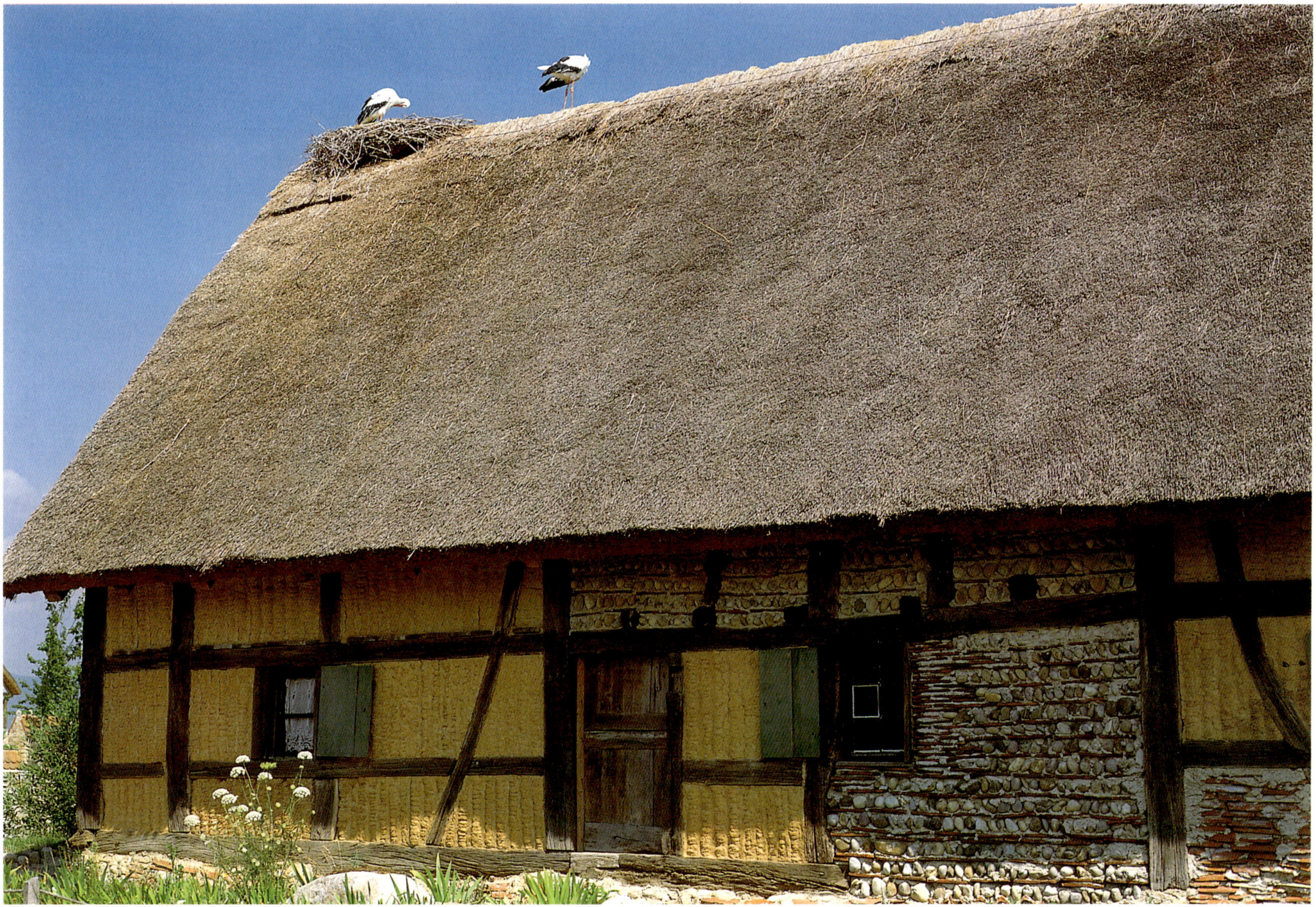

Ensisheim
Haut-Rhin

Centuries of development of timber-framed buildings in the Sundgau region produced simple, confident, entirely functional, yet very beautiful buildings with well-balanced proportions between timber and infill. The double-casement windows of this example in the Ensisheim Écomusée are separated just to the extent that their shutters do not overlap. The timber framework and its structural functions are clearly expressed on the façade. The superb 'beaver's tail' tiles – handmade flat clay tiles – effortlessly cover the roof. The infill between the timber frame is naturally coloured. The traditional and very satisfying pale blue on the windows and door is also used on the elegant gate to the kitchen and flower garden across the road.

Ensisheim
Haut-Rhin

This early eighteenth-century farmhouse in the Écomusée is sturdily constructed in a simple framework of oak with long, diagonal braces and short, paired braces called St Andrew's Crosses. An infill of daub, made up of the *torchis* mixture of puddled clay and chopped straw, is pushed into the framework from both the front and the back in a technique known as 'armoured daub'. The daub is scored while damp to give either a decorative finish as here or to provide a key for a protective lime and sand rendering called *kratzputz*. The sand of the Vosges gives a natural rosy hue while the sand from the Jura gives a yellow colour. In the seventeenth century this colour range was extended by the addition of oxide powders used in the dying of textiles. In some Alsatian villages a particular colour will predominate, such as blue in Bouxwiller, where the chemical dye *kelsch* was added.

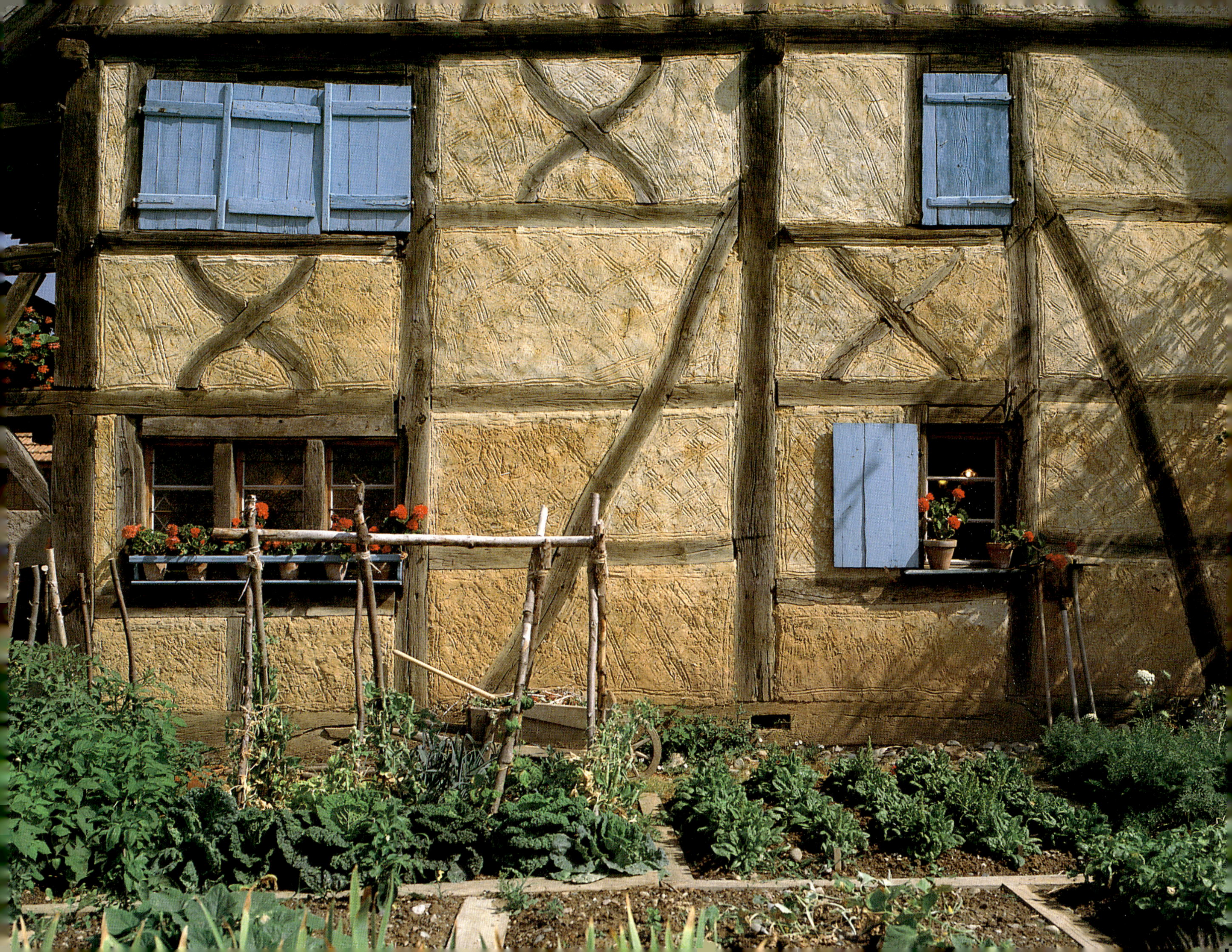

FRANCHE-COMTÉ

Grandfontaine
Doubs

Like ships about to go to sea these great farmhouses must take on board everything they will need for a voyage through the gales and the snow storms of a winter that can last for seven months of the year. The whole of the upper wooden superstructure is filled with hay and straw, since a well-stocked barn is essential for dairy cows that consume 4.5 kg (10 lb) of hay each a day. At the first icy blasts of winter the livestock are led inside. While the house was isolated in a sea of snow, it was said that if the stocks of hay were only half used up by 23 February all would be well. The animals would emerge on 25 May, the Feast of St Urban, often so weak and emaciated that the cows had to be helped to their feet. Two families used to live in these great farmhouses which took three years to build. Spruce and pine trees equivalent to the volume of the house would have been needed in the construction; 20,000 timber roof shingles alone were needed to cover the roof before the introduction of tiles.

Grandfontaine
Doubs

This eighteenth-century barn door, reached by a ramp up to the slope-facing gable end of the house opposite, is hung with long planks of wood called *lambrissures*. Wood will last for centuries if split with an axe or adze rather than sawn. This way it splits along the natural cleavage line, found between the soft, fast-growing spring and summer growth and the hard, slow-growing autumn and winter growth, and presents an unbroken and impenetrable layer of cells and fibres to the weather. Neither is it painted, since no paint will stand up to the range of temperatures found in the Alps. Left to itself, the wood becomes hard and rot-proof, with a surface furrowed by deep fibre lines where the lighter organic material of the summer growth has been dissolved between sharp ridges of pure cellulose. This is impregnated with a golden-brown-coloured, natural tar drawn to the surface of the wood by the sun's heat.

FRANCHE-COMTÉ

Les Rayières
Doubs

These large, square Haut-Doubs farmhouses are sheltered by a two-sided roof sweeping low to the ground to ensure the run-off of rain and melting snow. The barn takes up nearly the whole of the first floor and is entered by means of a ramp up to the *porte cochère* on the north-western façade. The gable end is clad with the vertical *lambrissure* boarding, which, like Yorkshire boarding, leaves a gap between boards to allow air to circulate through the barn. The chimney piercing the roof is the tip of a large plank-lined cone that at ground floor level occupies a space of some 5 square metres (54 sq.ft). This tall vertical space becomes a windowless kitchen – a kitchen within a chimney – commonly called a *tue* or *tuez*. In this high space bacon, ham, sausage, quarters of beef – a whole charcuterie – are hung to cure gently in the fragrant, rising smoke of pine and juniper. The external shutters covering the top of the *tuez* are called *vantaux* or *mantiaux* and are controlled internally by cords and chains. In the heavy snows of winter the *tuez* is sometimes the only way out of the building.

Chapelle-des-Bois
Doubs

This skilfully restored farmhouse (now a museum), with its projecting *tuez*, roof and gable end clad in larch shingles, was built in 1683. Its construction came after a ten-year-war between France and Spain when Swedish mercenaries destroyed most of the village while helping France to wrest control of the Jura from the Spanish. Curiously water shortage was a problem in this region of high rainfall because the Jurassic limestone absorbed it greedily and irretrievably. Consequently when such a house was built, the timber framework and roof with its cladding were built first. Rainwater was then collected off the roof by means of half-round larch-pole gutters which led to deep stone-built cisterns lined with puddled clay. Once these cisterns were full of water, the lime mortar could be made and the limestone walls built.

Lajoux
Jura

In the Jura the south-west brought the prevailing rain-bearing winds while the north-east brought the cold winds. The single-block farmhouses (*maisons blocs à terre*) were constructed with their gable ends facing these prevailing winds. In part this was to ensure that the winds regulated the amount of snow on the roof so that it did not become overloaded. The north-east end, although cold, was deemed the healthier end and here the family lived. The south-west end, with its problems of condensation and porous limestone walls (even though the best, carefully sorted and jointed stone was used), was where the animals were kept on the ground floor, while the large hay barn occupying most of the first floor was entered via an earth ramp and a round-arched *porte cochère*. The replacement, at the beginning of this century, of the original *tavillon* roof shingles with sheet metal destroyed part of the function of the rough wooden roof covering, since snow now slides off the roof and piles up round the doors and windows. The little, detached building on the right is a *grenier fort*, described opposite.

Lamoura
Jura

This little building clad in *tavillons* is a common sight in the mountains. Known as a *mazod* in Savoy and a *trésor* in Bresse, it is called a *grenier fort* here in the Haut-Jura. It is a small strengthened storehouse where the family kept their most treasured possessions and a reserve of food. Many reasons are given as to why they were built, but for me the most convincing is the peasant's obsessional fear of fire. These *greniers* were built in times when farmhouses were roofed by wood rafters covered by long wooden shingles (*anselles*); their roof spaces were immense and the floor was filled with straw and hay for use during long dark winters when candles, oil lamps and great roaring fires provided the only light. Farmhouses frequently went up in flames and burnt to the ground in minutes. The *grenier fort* was usually built on a dry, rocky promontory and often had a secret chamber cut into the rock under the floorboards.

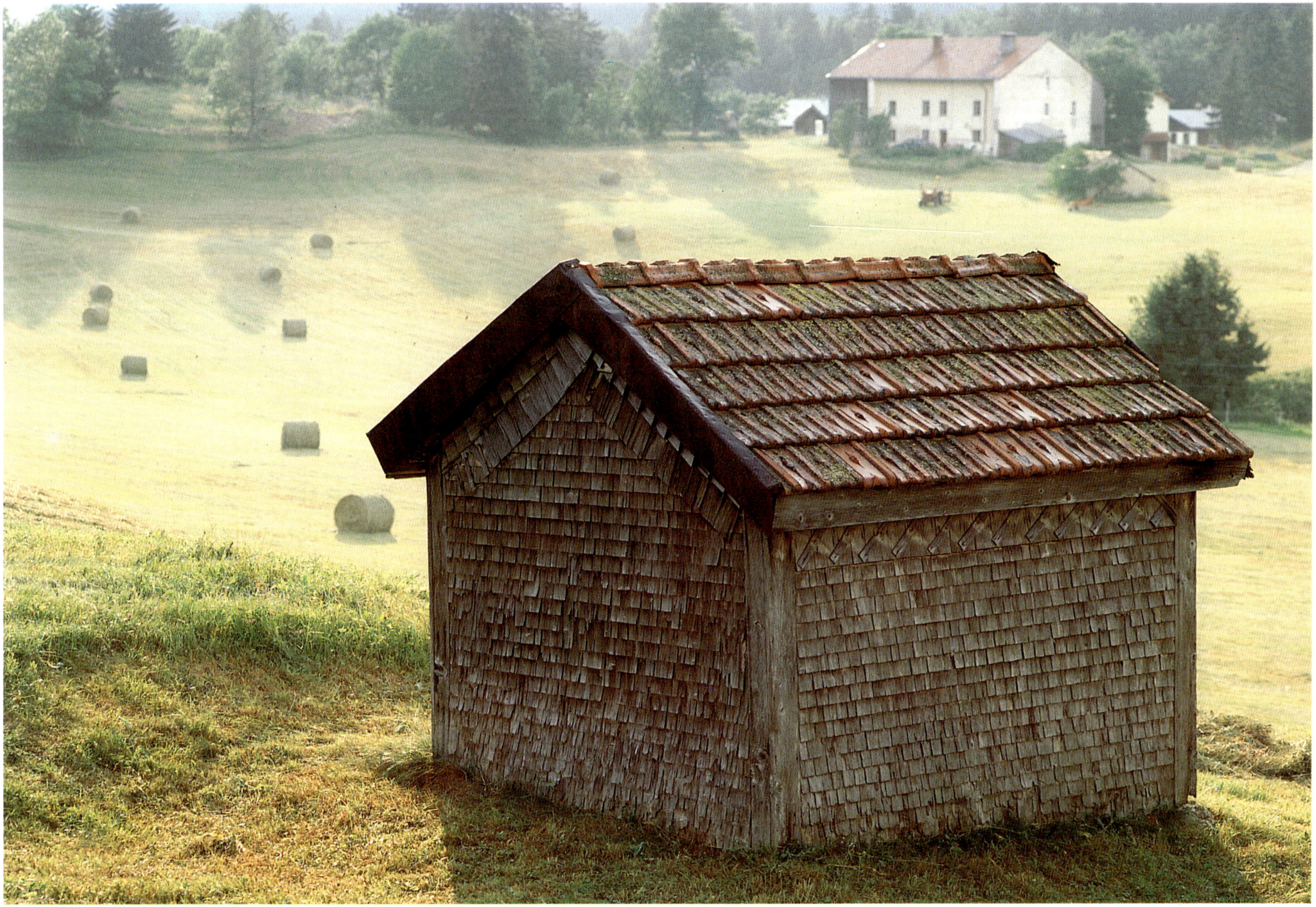

Lajoux
Jura

This farmhouse in the Jura has its exposed gable end protected by a vertical cladding of timber shingles (called *tavillons* in the Jura) and a small hipped roof, a *croupette*, to help the wind on its way. It is sited between its meadows and its mountain pastures. These permanent grasslands, lying over Jurassic limestone and untroubled by either fertilizers or herbicides, have developed an incredibly rich variety of wild flowers over the centuries. Visit the meadows in the month before the first hay cut in late May or early June – when they are scythed as close as the finest lawn – and you will see a profusion of wild daffodils, cornflowers, cinquefoils, yellow buttercups, cranesbills, orchids, white stars of Bethlehem and misty blue forget-me-nots. Higher still in the mountain pastures eager drifts of crocuses, pansies, anemones, violets, primroses, cowslips and gentians of the most intense blue appear even before the last of the snow has gone.

Les Forges de Syam
Jura

During the eighteenth century, and probably before, there was sufficient energy pent up in the River Ain to allow a forge to be established in this forested landscape of deep valleys. The growth and success of Les Forges de Syam, near Champagnole, was such that the forge masters and owners of this enterprise built an Empire mansion in the Palladian style for themselves. They also constructed for their workers this courtyard of tall terrace houses with its elegant central fountain. Built in Jurassic limestone with cut-stone dressings and a roof covered in fishscale tiles, the buildings flank a large arched entrance into the quadrangular forge. Today the forge employs and houses forty-five people and produces high-quality steel profiles to virtually any specification for export and home use. A high-technology business is carried out in buildings which have not changed since 1813, except for the installation of a rolling mill in 1903.

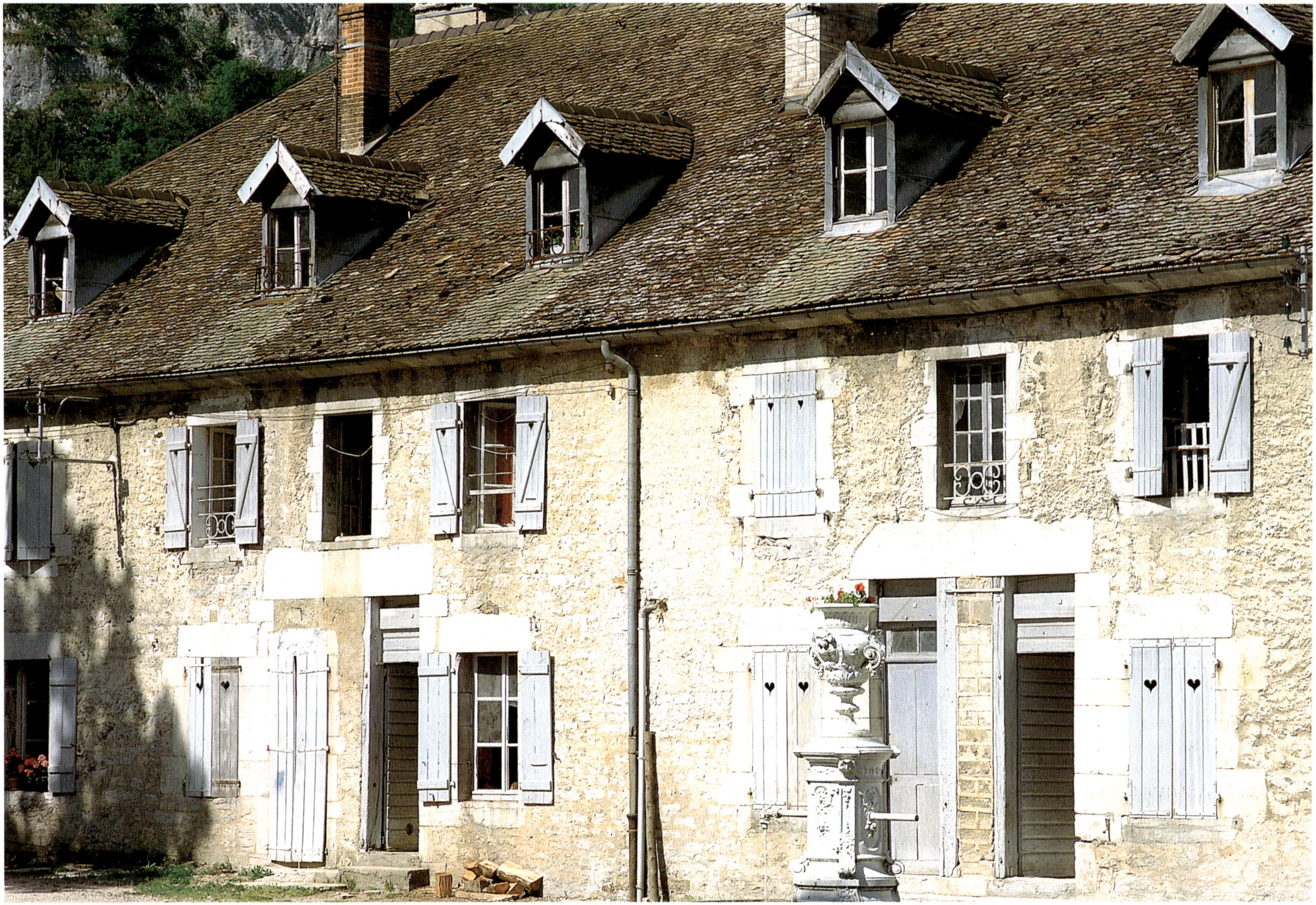

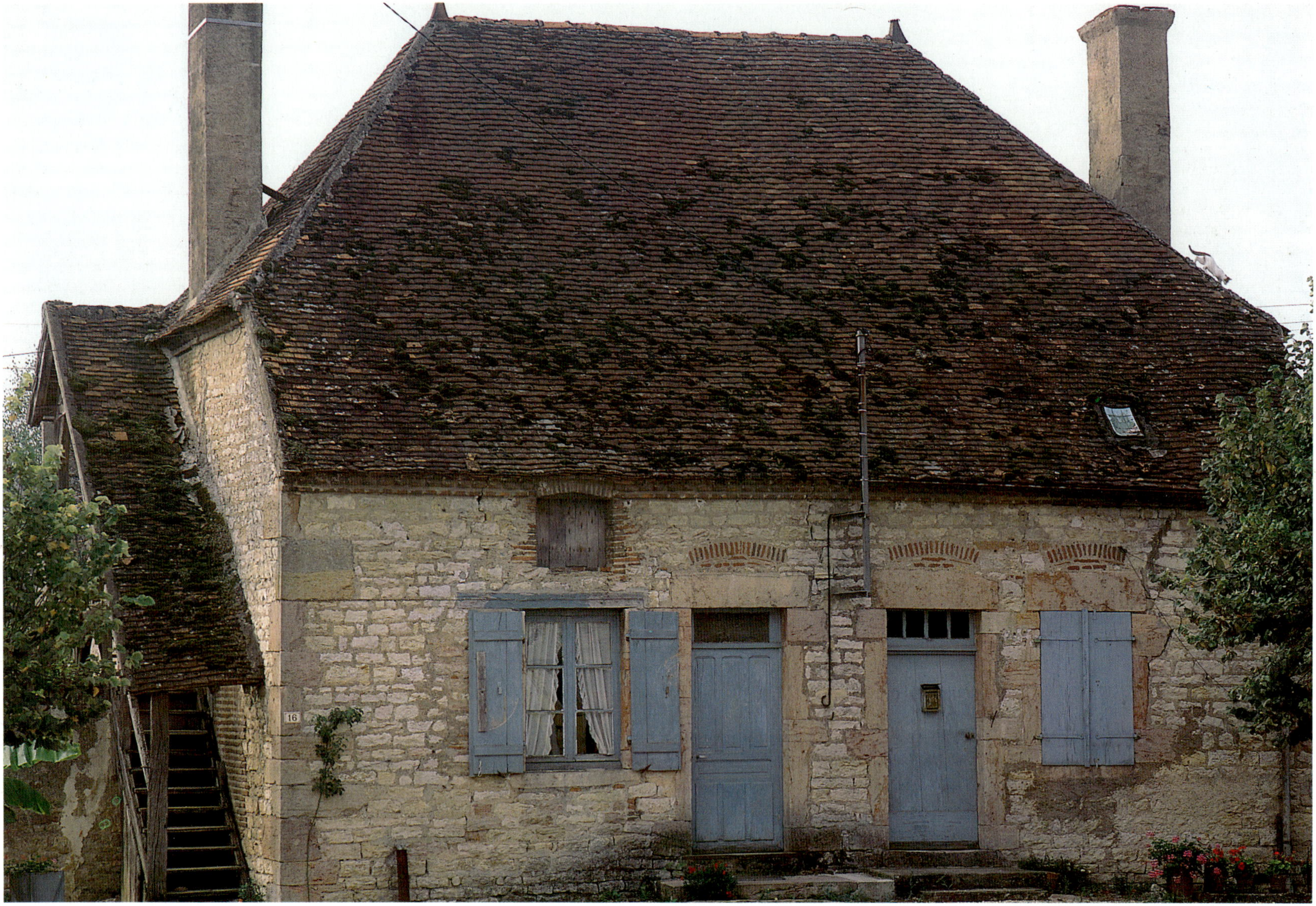
16

Mailly-le-Château
Côte-d'Or

In this simple semi-detached house for *journaliers* ('day labourers') there are two ground-floor rooms on each side, each with a loft above reached by a covered external staircase. A *four*, or bread oven, is built on the gable wall under the staircase. Coursed local limestone is used for the walls, strengthened by harder stone and brick at the corners and openings, including a brick relieving arch over the stone lintel to the door and corbelled brick eaves. Typically Burgundian is the steep, hipped roof of flat clay tiles, and the symmetry of the two dwellings is enhanced by the chimney on each gable wall and the terracotta finials at each end of the canal tile ridge.

Labergement-lès-Seurre
Côte-d'Or

This small village lies on the first rise of ground to the west of the marshy plains of the rivers Saône and Doubs. It is a farming community of small scattered parcels of land in a hedged landscape. The farms of the Saône practised mixed farming, where market and kitchen gardens and orchards enclosed the farming communities and the land beyond was given over to stock rearing, cereals and some vines. The photograph shows the principal south-facing façade of an eighteenth-century farmstead typical of the region. Flat clay tiles cover unequal pitched roofs, one of which, on the south-west side, sweeps almost to the ground over a stable, protecting the building from the prevailing wind. A framework of distinctive, closely spaced timber posts with diagonal braces supports the roof of the farmbuilding; the large entrance door to the barn can be seen with the smaller door to the stable on its left. Brick, recently rendered, is used for the walls of the farmhouse on the extreme right and for the infill of the farm buildings.

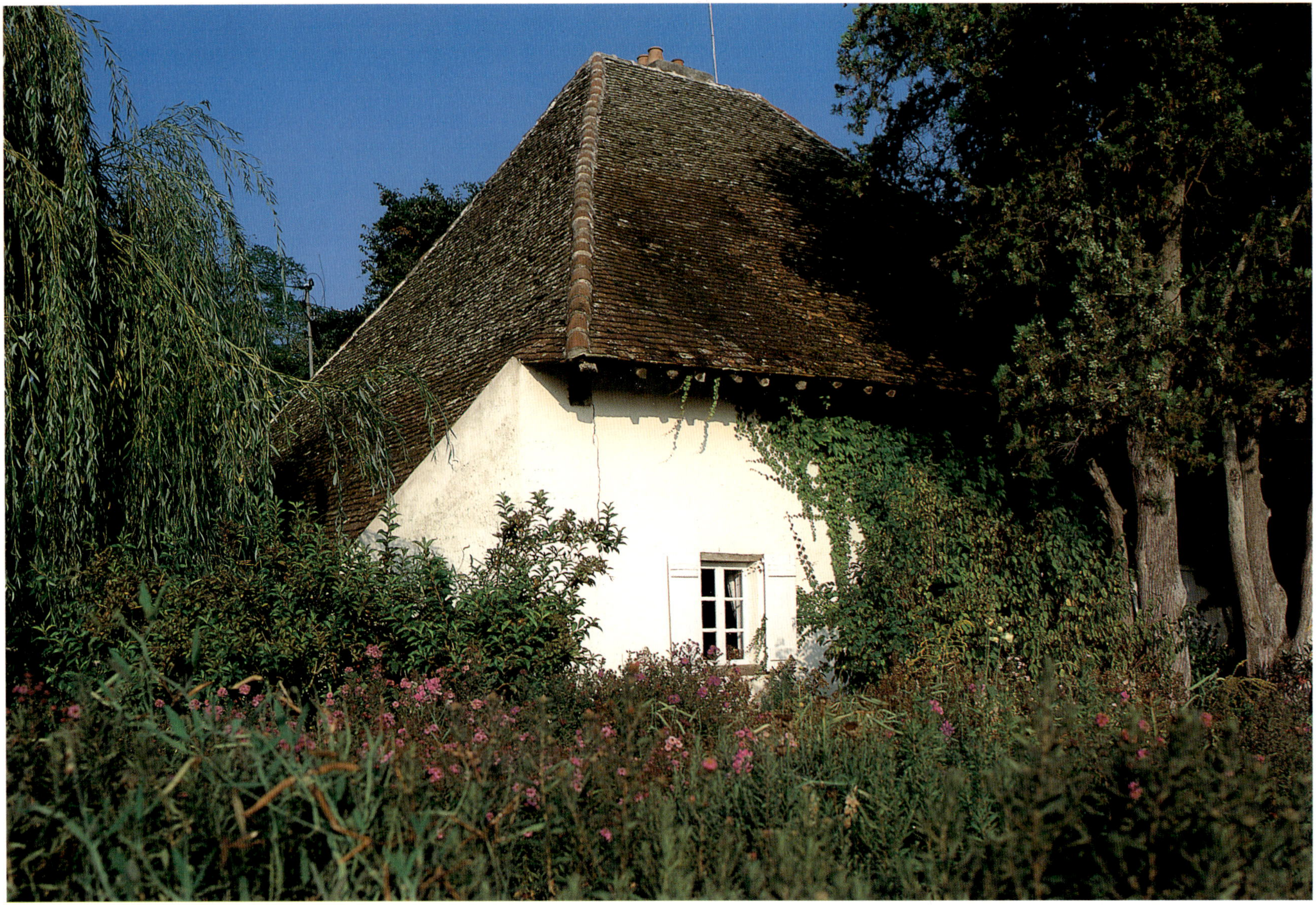

Saint-Symphorien-sur-Saône
Côte-d'Or

Steeply pitched, hipped roofs clad in small, flat tiles are characteristically Burgundian. The flat tile was first used in Burgundy by the Cistercian monks in the eleventh century to cover the steep roofs of their abbey buildings and was for a long time called the *tuile de Bourgogne*. The hip is here carried to the ground to shield the south-west elevation from the prevailing winds while the roof over the main sun-seeking south-eastern façade is projected forward at the eaves to protect walls commonly built of clay cob. It is a traditional design approach resulting in a comfortable-looking house at ease with itself and nearly lost in gardens which were once the main means of feeding the family.

Noiron
Saône-et-Loire

This symmetrically designed, stone-built farmhouse, with its farm buildings laid out alongside, was constructed in the eighteenth century, but the house was restored and the farm buildings converted to residential use in 1980. Although the farm is situated on the borders of Morvan and Burgundy, the architecture is clearly Burgundian. The stone lintels over the ground floor farmhouse windows have brick relieving arches since the tensile strength of the local stone was not trusted. The window on the left of the front door lights the kitchen, as beside it projects a *pierre à eau*, a large one-piece stone sink with a channel cut into it to take the waste water through the wall and clear of the building. Often you will find a small lozenge-shaped window called an *oeil de boeuf*, or 'bull's eye', just above the *pierre à eau* expressly there to light the sink.

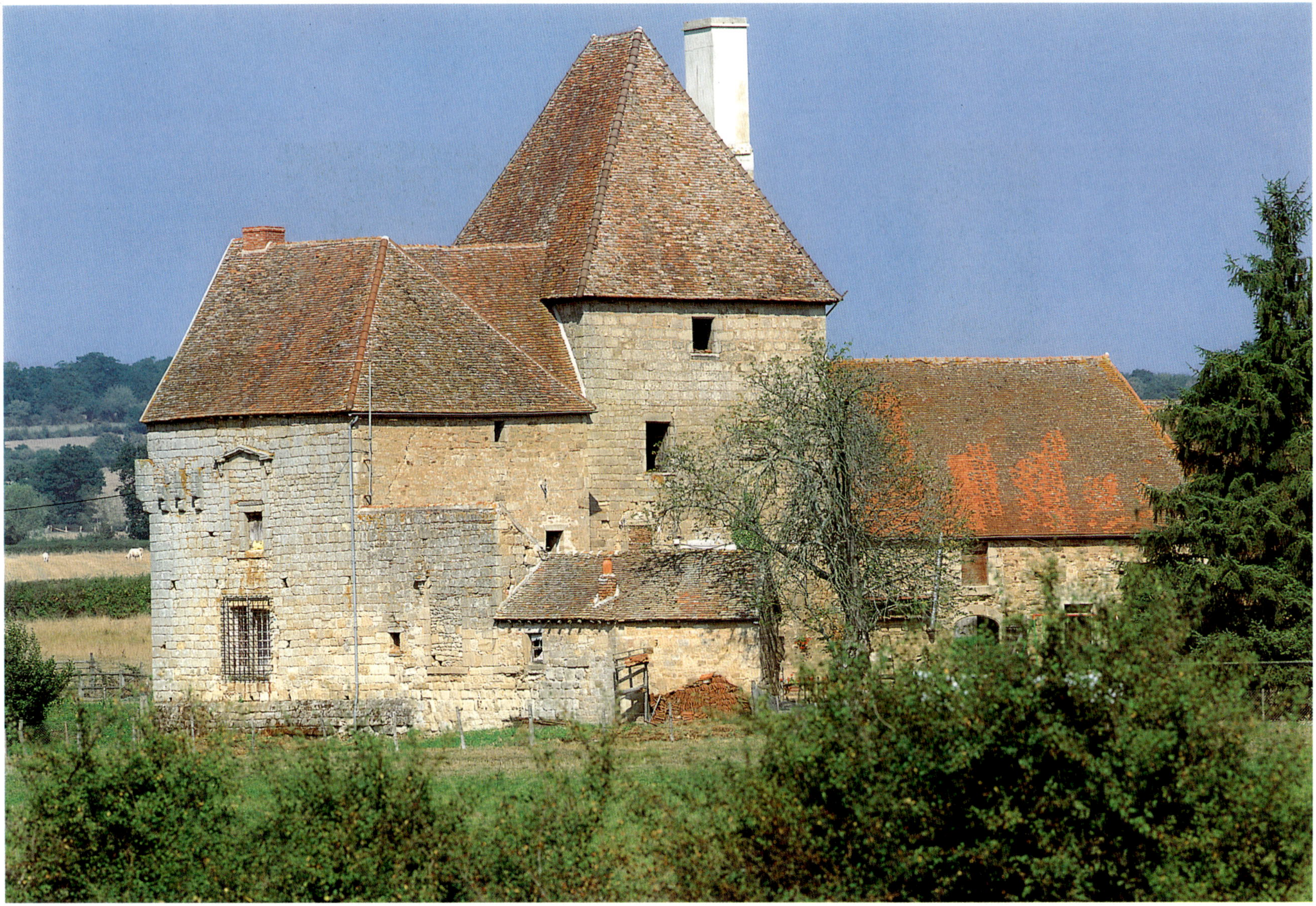

Lally
Saône-et-Loire

The decline in the power of the church and aristocracy after the French Revolution resulted in many churches, monasteries and châteaux being abandoned and then used as a source of building materials or as agricultural buildings. The little château of Lally, seen here, became a working farm in the nineteenth century but dates back to the twelfth century as a moated castle. It lies on flat fertile soils beside the River Lacanche, a tributary of the River Arroux which runs through the limestone foothills of the Morvan Regional Park, a granite massif which rises in the west to a height of over 900 m (3000 ft). The central three-storey donjon was built in the fifteenth century by Denis Poillot, president of the Parliament of Paris and French ambassador to the English court under Francis I. The steep-sided hipped roof replaced a crenellated terrace which originally capped the donjon. The remnants of corbels, once supporting machicolation, and traces of windows and pediments in the classical style suggest that this building has undergone several alterations.

Champsigny
Saône-et-Loire

This rendered and tiled nineteenth-century farmhouse has unusual, diamond-shaped pitch holes to the upper granary in the roof space. The farm is set within earlier fortifications which tell of a turbulent age when this area was part of a disputed Burgundian kingdom which stretched westwards to the Alps. The entrance gate with its white painted doors originally had a vertically closing portcullis and drawbridge, as can be seen from the machicolations and vertical openings of this solid stone structure with its coat of arms. It has been variously owned by Claude de Morey, secretary to the King and Chancellor of Navarre, who was created the Maquis de Vianges in 1723; and by Marie Edme Patrice, Comte de MacMahon, Duc de Magenta (1808–1893) and marshall and president of France from 1873 to 1879. It remains in the estate of the present Duc de Magenta.

Les Ecassas
Ain

The influence of Alsace, brought down the River Rhône, is shown in the use of clay fishscale tiles on the roof of this farmhouse, built by the river. However, the stepped coping on the gable, covering an extended internal wall, is a local feature called *pas d'oiseau* ('bird steps'), though it also occurs in the Cévennes and Pyrenees, where it is known as *pas de moineau* ('sparrow steps'). It is constructed of stone slabs, each slightly inclined downwards to throw rainwater off, and betrays the former use of thatch. The raised gable end protected the vulnerable edge of a thatch roof from wind damage, while the stone steps sat on long spars, which held the thatch-reed, straw, heather or broom in place, and the steps themselves were designed to give access to the roof for maintenance work. The nearness and influence of the south is shown in the canal tile ridge.

Saint-Genest-Malifaux
Loire

The Pilat Regional Park is centred on Mont Pilat, a sharply rising pyramid of a mountain with massive crests at around 1400 m (4,600 ft), which support extensive forests of ash, chestnut, beech and pine and a few pastures. It is an area of distinct regions, each with its own traditions and architecture. The farmsteads of the Saint-Genest-Malifaux plateau date from the nineteenth century, having developed in parallel with the industrial revolution taking place in nearby Saint-Étienne. The farmhouses are narrow and high with the family living on two floors linked by a central staircase. Characteristic of this vernacular tradition are the nine openings in the façade, symmetrically arranged and getting smaller as they go up. Adjoining farm buildings are built either as a continuation of the farmhouse or at right-angles to it, as here. The cowshed is at ground level while above is the barn, reached by an earth ramp known as a *montoir*. The canal tiles of the Mediterranean combine with the granite walls of the Massif Central in this transition area.

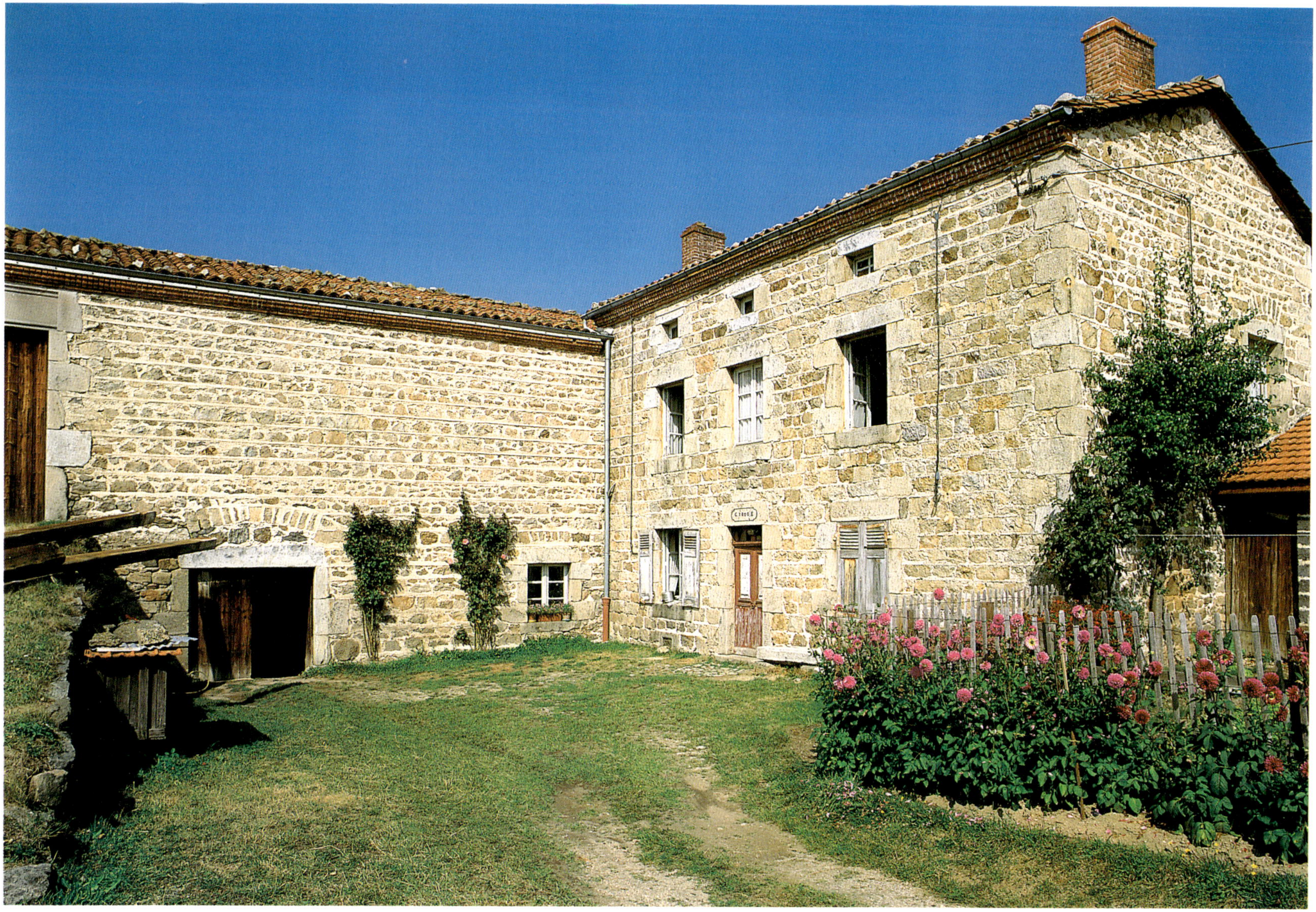

SAVOY

L'Ecot
Savoie

Slabs of gneiss, orange with lichen in these high, unpolluted airs, are scattered across the low-pitched roofs of these summer chalets in the hamlet of L'Ecot. The chalets face south-east into the sun. Their ridges point south-westwards towards the Massif de la Vanoise and into the prevailing wind. By huddling together and shuffling their gable ends up to one another, each house protects the other, while the spinal curve they describe shields the street from the searching wind. The number of chalets and hamlets dotted about the High Alps gives a wrong impression of the population, as people were always on the move in local migrations called *remues*. The permanent village lay on a lower plateau but in the spring its people drove their flocks and herds up to the *montagnette*, the meadows freshly emerged from the snow, to live in hamlets such as L'Ecot. As snow melted the animals would be taken further up to the *montagne*, the mountain pastures, where the herdsmen would live for two or three months in more primitive chalets.

L'Ecot
Savoie

When Christianity reached these remote areas, a religious centre had to be established in each of the high isolated valleys, and there is a diocese here in the Tarentaise region to this day. The people who occupied these valleys had to move in an annual migration up and down the mountains in search of grass for their flocks and herds, and their religion, which was an integral part of their way of life, required them to attend mass on Sundays and holy days. As a result, chapels, like this one high in the mountains of the Haute-Maurienne, were built at each point of their annual migration. The sound of its single bell measured the day, calling the peasants to prayer and mingling with the sound of sheep bells and cow bells in an otherwise silent landscape.

Bonneval-sur-Arc
Savoie

The village of Bonneval-sur-Arc is situated at an altitude of 1835 m (6,000 ft), at the foot of the Col de l'Iseran. In this house stone voussoirs arch over the entrance to the stable. Beside it the large spruce doors give access to the capacious storage space needed to ensure survival over the long winter. The roof with its stone *lauzes* projects forward to cover the drying balcony. The protective timber railings are charmingly called *garde fou*, which perhaps translates as 'guard against foolishness' or 'guard for fools'.

Vincendières
Savoie

Situated in the Vallée d'Avérole, Vincendières is one of four hamlets of Bessans. Its wide-pitched roofs covered in heavy stone *lauzes* project over galleries extending the full width of the house. The balcony was used to store brushwood, firewood and, in an area short of wood, a fuel called *terre pétrie*, made from earth and hay kneeded together with the binding help of cow manure and then dried. Here also was hung maize, beans, hemp and washing. Most of the living accommodation is on the ground floor but bedrooms are also to be found on the first floor. The hamlet was the birthplace in the seventeenth century of Jean Clappier, the head of a dynasty of wood sculptors whose work is still to be seen in the shrines cut into the walls of villages and in isolated rocks beside the valley roads.

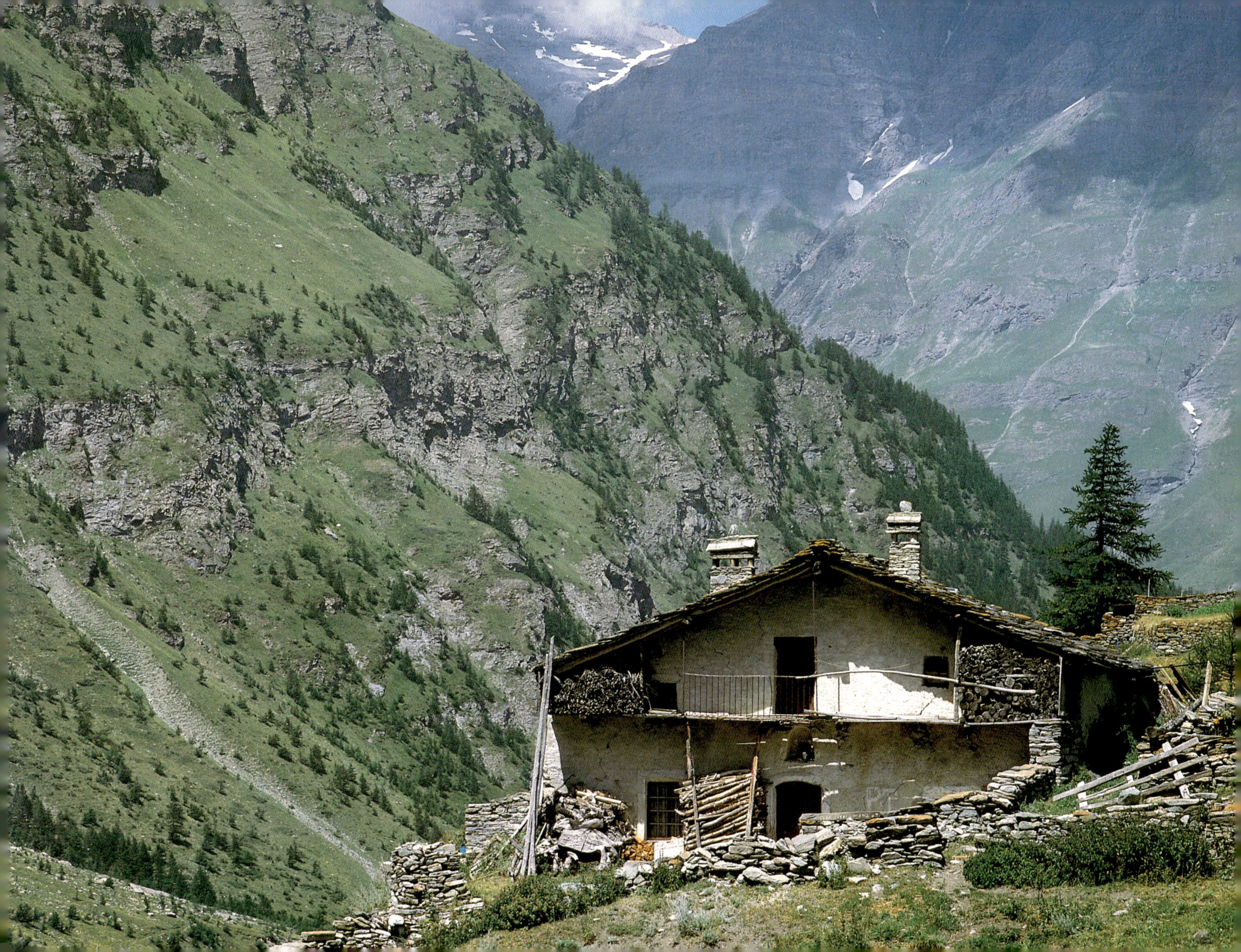

Le Laus
Hautes-Alpes

Called *essendoles*, the timber roof coverings of this farm building are bigger and longer than the otherwise similar *tavaillons* and were made in the Hautes-Alpes from split, not sawn, larch or Norway spruce. Elsewhere chestnut was used and more rarely beech and oak. The larch and spruce were preferably selected from the shaded side of the mountain where the trees grew more slowly and the wood was consequently more densely grained. The selected trees were felled in the last quarter of November on a day without frost. Made in this way, *essendoles* can last for a century. Here, the roof extends over a timber-drying balcony for the adjacent hay-storage area on the upper floor, and rainwater is caught by timber gutters – half-round hollowed-out poles – carried on timber brackets.

La Chau
Hautes-Alpes

Those who built in this harsh landscape of ice and rock have met like with like by taking the stone and the wood about them and making a carapace for themselves and their animals which both reflects and combats the hard world outside. Family and animals would live together behind thick protective walls on the ground and first floor, insulated by the hay-filled loft above them. This upper story is clad with vertical boarding, and the steeply pitched roof is covered with boards of spruce or larch called *essendoles*, which direct water down into hollowed-out larch-pole gutters. In these mountain fastnesses the peasant family and their animals would hibernate, riding out the howling winds and blinding blizzards of winter.

PROVENCE

Saint-Véran
Hautes-Alpes

Like a line of sunflowers, the chalets of Saint-Véran with their open first-floor galleries all face the southern sun along a 2,040 m (6,700 ft) contour line high above the Vallée de l'Aigue Blanche. It is the highest village in Europe or, as it is said in the local dialect, *Saint-Véran es la plus aouto mountagno onte se mandjo de pan* ('Saint-Véran is the highest mountain where bread is eaten'). It is also the only village in the Queyras region named after a saint, because he delivered the area from a nasty dragon. Believing you can only take Christian charity so far, Saint Véran (bishop of the area) told the dragon to 'fly off', or words to that effect. The dragon did so to everyone's surprise and possibly his own, not expecting a bishop to speak like that, for he crashed into the mountains killing himself. The demise of the dragon was reported by shepherds coming up from Provence and the people of Queyras rejoiced by building a village on the spot and naming it after their saintly bishop. This legend underlines the ancient relationship of transhumance (seasonal migration) between the Midi and Saint-Véran.

Saint-Véran
Hautes-Alpes

This upper, northern façade of a typical farm building shows the entrance to the first-floor barn, with underneath the stone-built ground floor, which the peasant family shared with their animals during the hard winter. At the back of the barn, marked externally by the projecting larch poles of the internal dividing wall, is the family's summer quarters, fronted on the south by a wide projecting balcony, with a *grenier* above. The larch poles of the upper-storey walls are crossed and half-housed one into the other at the corners. Larch poles are also used as rafters, spanning the length rather than the width of the farmhouse to support the roof projections over the balcony and the barn entrance. Split lengths of larch (*essendoles*) cover the main roof, and a special ridge design directs rainwater into timber gutters which project well clear of the building. The shallower lower roof on the left is covered with thin schist *lauzes*, whose corners are pointed down-slope to assist water run-off. The traditionally designed stone chimneys with their protective copings are an attractive feature of the area.

Saint-Véran
Hautes-Alpes

Les cadrans solaires, 'sundials', are a remarkable feature of the high mountain villages of Queyras. Sadly, as they are no longer the main way of telling the time, they have been neglected and often thoughtlessly damaged. They are painted on walls, and sometimes two are put together on adjoining walls so that one receives the rays of the rising sun and the other the rays of the setting sun. Artists, like the Italian Giovanni Francesco Zarbuli who worked in the Queyras region between 1833 and 1870, specialized in and signed these works. They were colourfully decorated with geometric patterns, flowers and birds – here, for instance, a toucan and a flycatcher (*gobe-mouche*) – and dated. They were also often given delightful inscriptions, which expressed both religious devotion and a sense of the transitory, precarious nature of life, such as 'without the sun I am nothing but, as for you, without God you can achieve nothing' or the splendid '*la vie n'est pas grand chose, un rire, un souffle, une larme*' ('life is no big thing, a laugh, a breath, a tear').

Saint-Martin-de-la-Brasque
Vaucluse

The Montagne du Lubéron, part of the Petites Alpes de Provence, rises high above this Provençal *mas*, the name given to farmsteads in the Midi, sheltering it from the strong-blowing mistral winds that tear down the Rhône valley. With or without such mountainous protection Provençal farmhouses present a closed face to these northern winds, keeping the doors and windows for their southern façades. Here would be the main entrance to the *pièce à vivre* – the living room, dining room, kitchen and bedroom all in one. Generally the Provençal peasant was involved in small-scale farming in order to feed himself and a usually numerous family. He produced wheat, oats and vegetables; he cultivated vines and olive trees; and he had a mule, a few sheep, some goats and a farmyard. In the best situations he also had a few cows and a *pigeonnier*. Here the *pigeonnier* (on the left) is a typical Provençal dovecot with a single-pitch, canal-tile roof sloping southward and a parapet wall on all other sides to give protection from the prevailing winds.

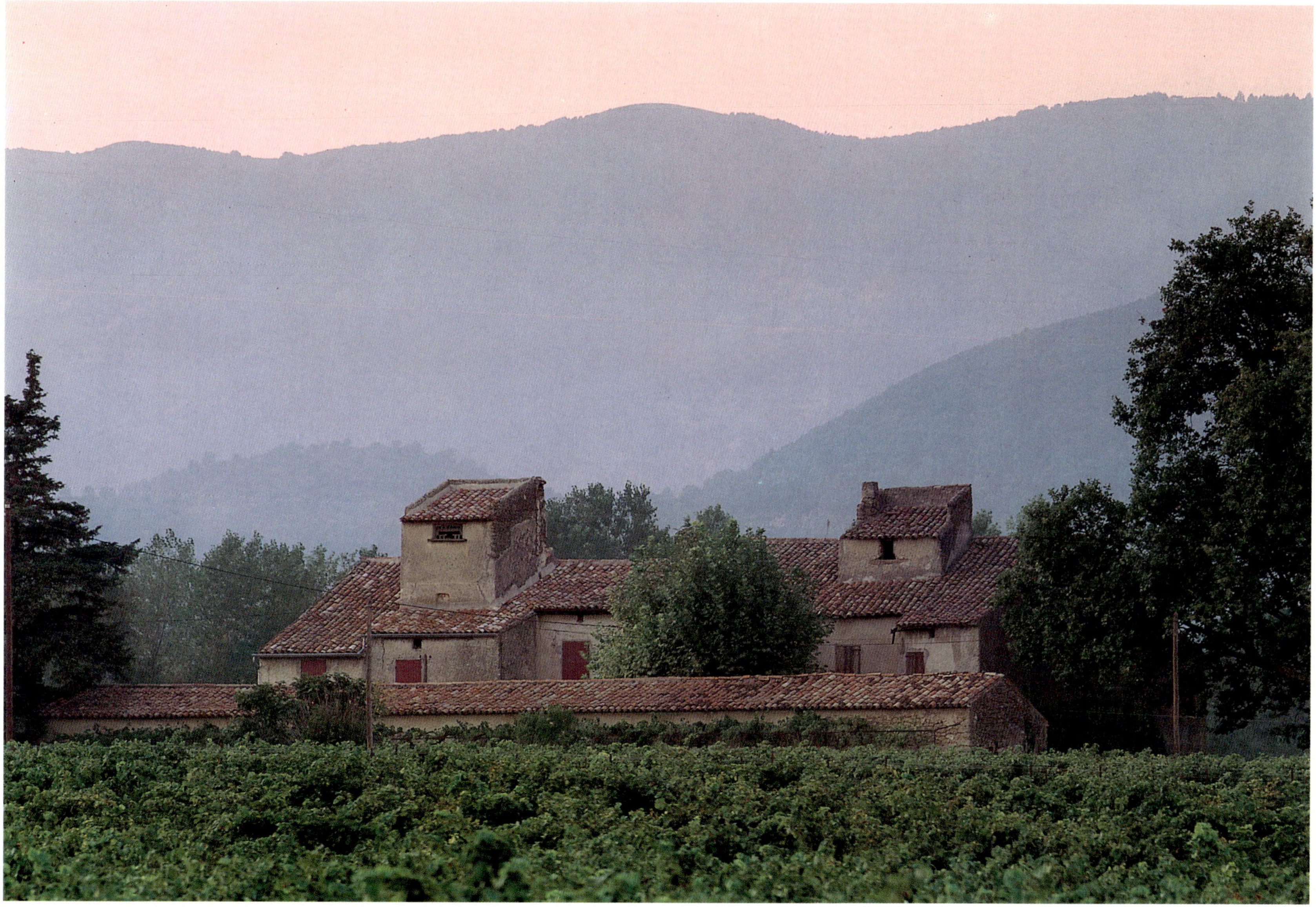

Lauris
Vaucluse

This Provençal farmhouse, with its air of immovable solidity, makes a simple, strong statement in a hot dry landscape. The rendered stone walls have a monolithic appearance, with openings that seem to be punched reluctantly and randomly into its sides. Shallow-pitched roofs are clamped tightly onto the walls by means of a *génoise* – a series of corbelled canal tiles at the eaves which support the projecting roof – and the chimneys are short and stubby. It is a bastion against the ferocity of the summer sun and presents no weakness, no slender projections on which the mistral wind can test its strength. The soft red-and-yellow ochres of the roofs and walls blend perfectly with the rich green of the dwarf oak forest that surrounds them and with the single wind-firm Cyprus tree that keeps the building company.

Roussillon
Vaucluse

Perched at an altitude of 335 m (1,100 ft), this Lubéron village rises dramatically above sheer cliffs of deep red sandstone called *Les Falaises de sang et d'or* ('Cliffs of blood and gold'). Here ochre, a mixture of sandy clays and oxide, was quarried right up to the village itself. The quarried ochre was placed in running water to wash out the sands, and the remaining ochre clay was then dried, cut into blocks and ground into powder. It was produced in seventeen different hues from red to yellow and used as a paint pigment until replaced by synthetic colouring agents in the 1950s. The use of ochre in the building trade gave Provence its distinctive colour renders, which do not fade in the fierce southern sun. These are nowhere displayed with such flamboyance and *joie de vivre* as in Roussillon itself, where even the twelfth-century Romanesque church with its square tower, sundial and wrought-iron bell cage (whose bell is often rung by the mistral wind) is not too proud to receive a good coat of ochre render.

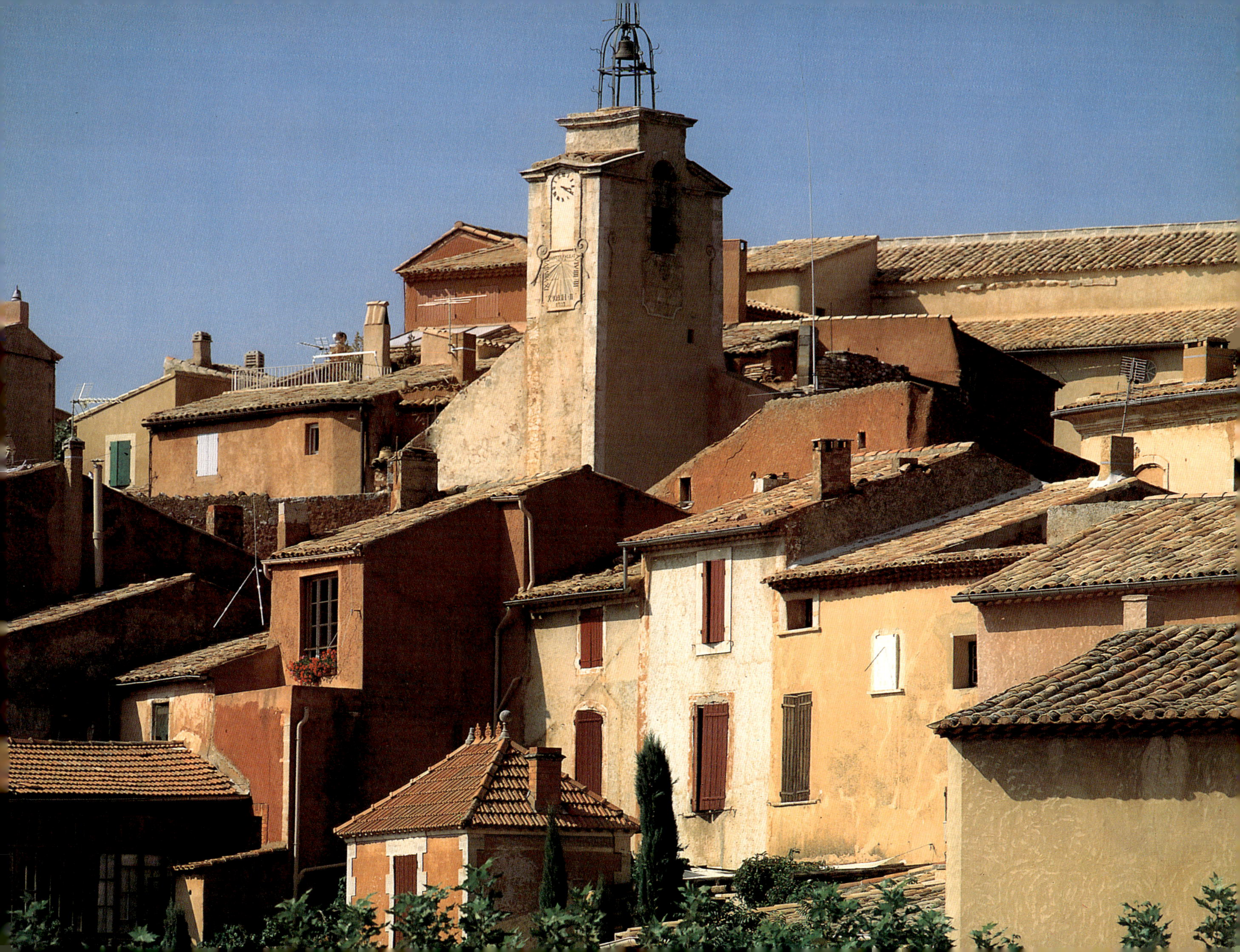

PROVENCE

Gordes
Vaucluse

The crisp, clean outline of a substantial *mas* is sharpened by the Mediterranean light and the dark green frame of the *garrigue*-covered hills. The *garrigue* is a dry, thin-soiled scrub of dwarf, deciduous and evergreen oaks (the Languedoc term for the evergreen kermes oak – *garric* – gives the area its name), broom, aspic lavender, cotton cistus and sweet-smelling herbs, which probably appeared after the destruction of the oak forests that once covered the uplands of this area. This destruction was the result of over-exploitation from Roman times onwards, compounded by fires, the ravages of browsing herds of sheep and goats and topsoil run-off. These losses were recognized in the seventeenth century when measures were taken to protect the remaining woodland. Peasants were given a duty to sow acorns, to build dry-stone retaining walls called *restanques*, to stop topsoil run-off and to use timber in a limited and simplified way in buildings. This is reflected in the vernacular architecture with its narrow, short-span roofs requiring only basic, shallow-depth rafters – a style that can be seen in this courtyard farmstead.

Gordes
Vaucluse

The flat surface stone so plentiful in the limestone area of Provence, as here in the Lubéron Regional Park, has been used over the centuries by the peasants and shepherds to build dry-stone walls, terraces and shelters called *bories*. Built for themselves, their animals and their tools, these shelters were round, rectangular or oval with neither chimney nor window, and their roofs (called *toitures*) were corbelled inwards to form a dome. Their origins are unknown but they have been a feature of this landscape for as long as man has inhabited it. These three *bories* – *pigeonniers* known as the Trois Soldats, or 'three soldiers' – are unique of their type and stand on a ridge of olive trees just below Gordes on the D2. They were constructed in 1860 and were originally crowned by a *Titeia*, a Provençal term for a phallic doll used as a fertility symbol.

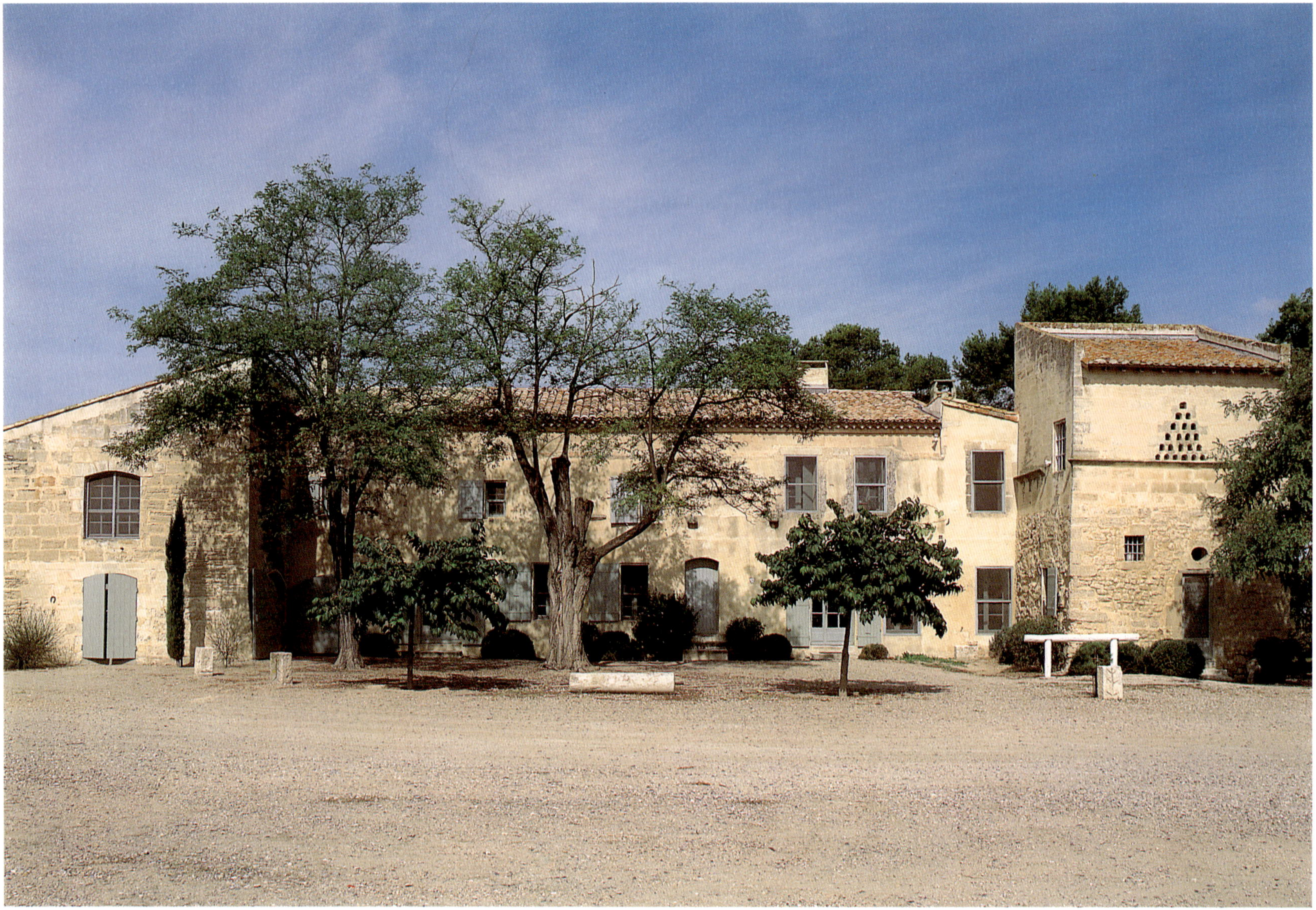

Mas du Pont de Rousty
Bouches-du-Rhône

The Camargue – the salt marshes of the Rhône delta – was historically divided into large estates called *mas*. These, like the Mas du Pont de Rousty here, managed their land in a number of concentric circles centred on the *mas*. The inner circle comprised vast kitchen gardens and orchards watered in summer from deep wells. Cultivation of wheat, rice and vines took place in the central ring of alluvial soil, while the outer ring of salt marshes was given over to grazing by the Camargue horses and black cattle, hunting, fishing and reed harvesting. The picture shows only a small number of the south-facing farm buildings, which were constructed in 1850. The cowshed with barn above is on the left, the *logis* or living area, is in the centre and a large and typically Provençal single-pitch *pigeonnier* is on the right. An immensely long *bergerie* is located just out of picture on the right. Here sheep were housed in winter and lambed in spring before being walked in the transhumance, or seasonal migration, 300 km (185 miles) up to the Alpine massif of Vercors in the summer.

Mas de Cacharel
Bouches-du-Rhône

If the Mas du Pont de Rousty represents the top of the social hierachy in the Camargue, a *cabane* like this represents the bottom. In these simple dwellings lived fishermen, agricultural workers, willow-cutters, shepherds, salt-workers, reed-cutters and particularly the *gardians* (Camargue herdsmen) for the practically wild, black cattle and grey horses, which roamed the salt marshes. The apse-like end of the *cabane* faced north and was designed to cope with the mistral. A chimney was built into the southern gable end beside the entrance door, which opened into either a single room or more commonly two rooms – a bedroom in the apse and a living-room in the southern end. Large families lived in these cramped quarters and not surprisingly they tended to cook, eat and live outdoors as much as possible. The roof, and often the walls as well, were constructed of the locally abundant reed, which on the ridge, walls and apsidal end was coated in thick layers of lime mortar. The slope of the apsidal end was usually topped by a wooden cross.

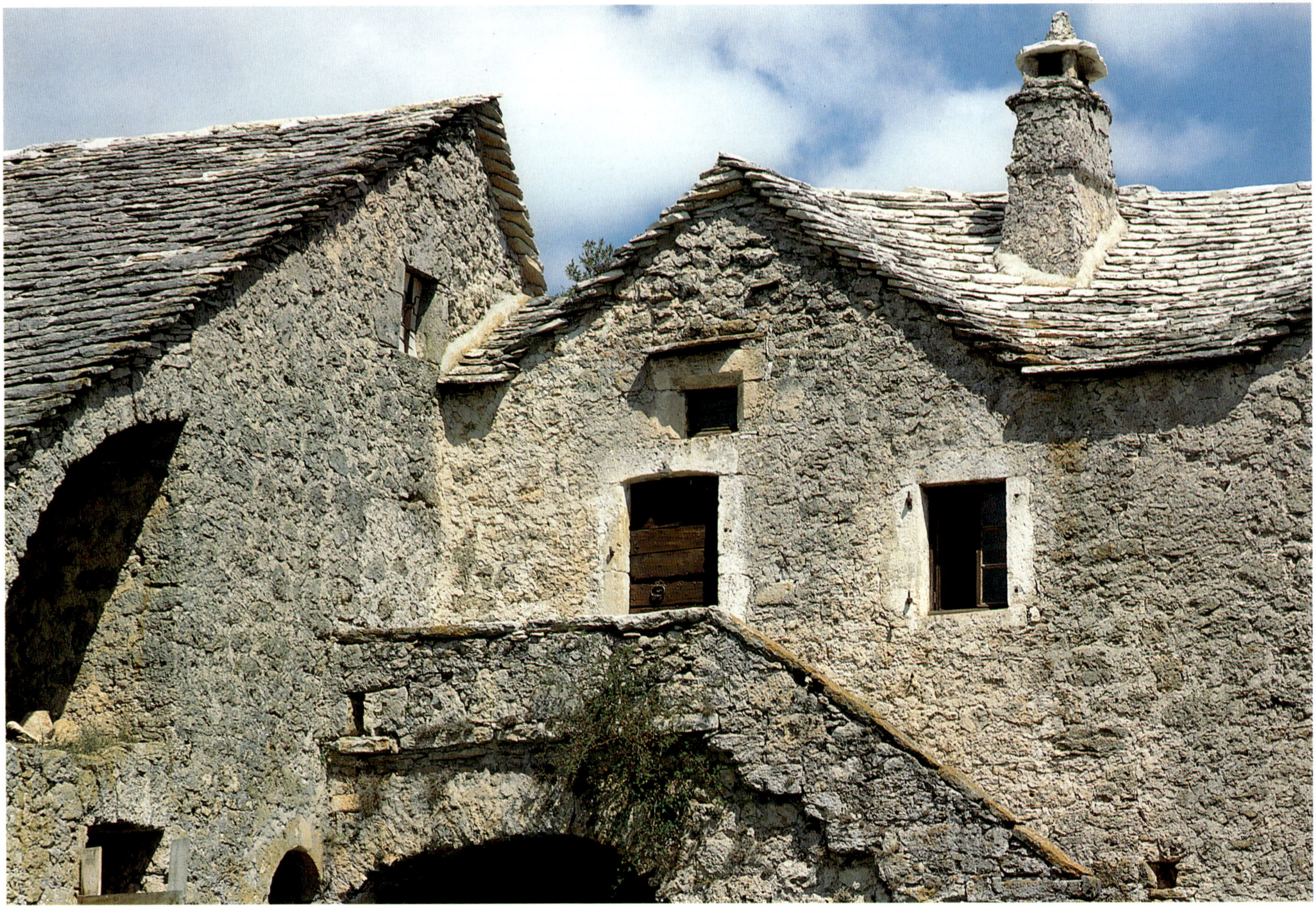

Saint-Pierre-des-Tripiers
Lozère

This tiny hamlet by the deep gorge of the Tarn can be found on the highest of the Grands Causses plateaux – a bare, thin-soiled limestone area grazed by sheep and watched over by birds of prey. But in spite of its stark appearance, the plateau was formerly a granary for the valleys. Its farm architecture reflects two basic facts about the area: the lack of trees and the lack of available water. The first problem was answered by using the very versatile and readily available limestone and making extensive barrel vaults to carry roofs, floors and upper-storey window openings (as here). The second problem was often overcome by leading wooden rainwater gutters inside to discharge into internal stone cisterns constructed as an inner skin to the external walls. Even so, water was scarce and flocks had to make do with rainwater collected in the clay *dolines*, which acted much like the dew ponds found on the English Downs. The external flight of stone steps, rising over the vaulted entrance to the sheepfold, leads up to a summer patio and the first-floor living quarters.

Saint-Pierre-des-Tripiers
Lozère

This barn (attached to the house opposite) is constructed entirely of limestone, with limestone vaults carrying the roof and the openings. The limestone slabs on the roof are immensely heavy and are laid without fixings on a bed of lime mortar. Today the local economy is based on sheep- and goat-rearing but it was at its height in the eighteenth century when the valleys of the Cévennes produced a large proportion of French silk. In the middle of the nineteenth century this traditional economy was hit by silk-worm disease. Louis Pasteur's discoveries later in the century overcame this problem but no answer was found to the competition posed by synthetic textiles early in the twentieth century. This, together with poor agricultural prices, resulted in a mass rural exodus, such that in 1970 only 500 people were left in the whole of the Cévennes National Park.

LANGUEDOC-ROUSSILLON

Troubat
Lozère

In the north of the Cévennes National Park the bare granite peak of Mont Lozère projects above an area of extensive peat-bogs and close-cropped turf littered with granite rocks. The farm buildings here have an air of sobriety and solidity whilst their use of the local pink granite ensures they melt into their landscape. In this example the mullioned windows and curved stone corbels supporting a projecting roof suggest some wealth. The farm buildings return on the right to give a classic 'L' shape to the farmstead. The walls are built with an internal and an external face regularly linked and stabilized by through-stones and by particularly large stones used in the foundations and at the corners. The internal space between the two faces is filled with *tout-venant* – any small stones that came to hand – mixed with clay to assist waterproofing of the walls. In a characteristic detail called *rastel*, the schist *lauzes* covering the roof are notched and housed into each other to form a weatherproof ridge to the building.

Troubat
Lozère

Roof coverings of schist *lauzes* glint in the sun. The roof around the apsidal bakehouse in the background dated 1851 is beautifully built in diminishing courses. Adjoining it is a pigsty and nearby the entrance to a threshing floor with 1781 carved into the lintel. All these buildings are linked together internally to the cowshed, barn and living quarters (pictured opposite) to save the peasant family from having to go outside during the harsh winters. Farmsteads on Mont Lozère at 1350 m (4,450 ft) are among the highest in the Massif Central.

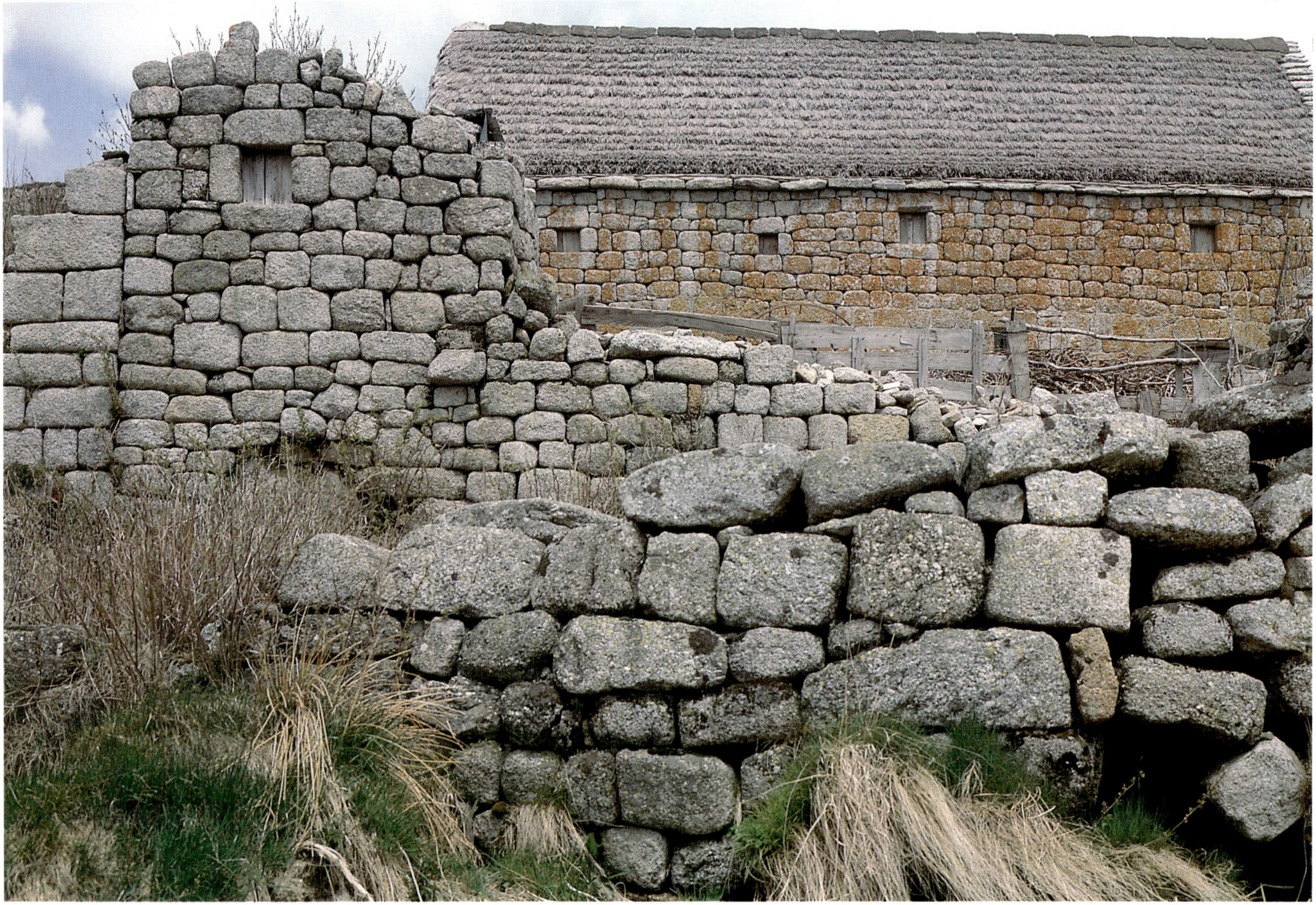

L'Hôpital
Lozère

Schist *lauzes* began to replace rye thatch in the Mont Lozère area in the seventeenth century. The rye was a local variety with long stalks cultivated for the purpose. Starting from the eaves, small bundles were laid in horizontal lines along the roof and tied with boiled beech twigs to horizontal spars of pine or oak underneath. Timber over-spars were then laid on top of them but were not visible because they were covered by the next line of bundles. These spars were held down by *pas de moineau* ('sparrow steps'), which were step-like slabs of granite capping the gables. The top lines of rye bundles on each pitch were folded across one another to form the ridge. However, to make the ridge more waterproof either another row of bundles was laid along the ridge and held down by stones or the ridge was covered by turf. Once in place, the thatch was combed smooth to a thickness of about 300 mm (1 ft). A hectare of land (2½ acres) was needed to grow sufficient rye to cover the average roof.

Les Bondons
Lozère

Ardèche is the foremost producer in France of farm-made goat cheese, and the sound of goat and sheep bells float over its hills. Constant grazing of these areas of the Cévennes has resulted in a treeless landscape and an architecture which has relied on stone to replace wood. On the limestone plateaux – the *causses* – roofs and openings are carried on stone arches and vaults, and within these areas further distinctive styles have grown up. Les Bondons lies in a locality known for its *lucarnes caussenardes*, vaulted dormers that run under the eaves of the limestone *lauze* roofs.

Les Badieux
Lozère

The architecture of this farmhouse built in 1809 reflects its geological situation between the granite of Mont Lozère and the limestone of the Causse Mejean and the Causse de Sauveterre. The walls are built of skilfully assembled, undulating courses of large, rough-cut granite blocks with extremely fine joints. The dormer windows, however, are typical of the *lucarnes caussenardes*, as seen at Les Bondons (previous page), which grew out of the vault and arch architecture of the limestone *causses*. The roof is covered in limestone *lauzes* carried well clear of the walls by granite corbels. The dry-stone walls are also built with the more workable limestone.

Les Badieux
Lozère

Without exception granite was quarried on the spot. It does not lie in beds as do schists and limestones but in massive irregular lumps. The mason would 'ring' the stone with a metal hammer to learn its points of weakness and work on these points with wedges until the stone split. Stones of all sizes from the cyclopean downwards were used either in roughly horizontal beds or in an irregular design without apparent organization but always achieving perfect cohesion. Here in unpolluted air the walls are covered in grey, black and orange lichens, which help prevent the penetration of water through the fine joints. Openings are small in proportion to the walls, and in some cases just three courses of granite can be as high as a man, creating a stunning visual effect.

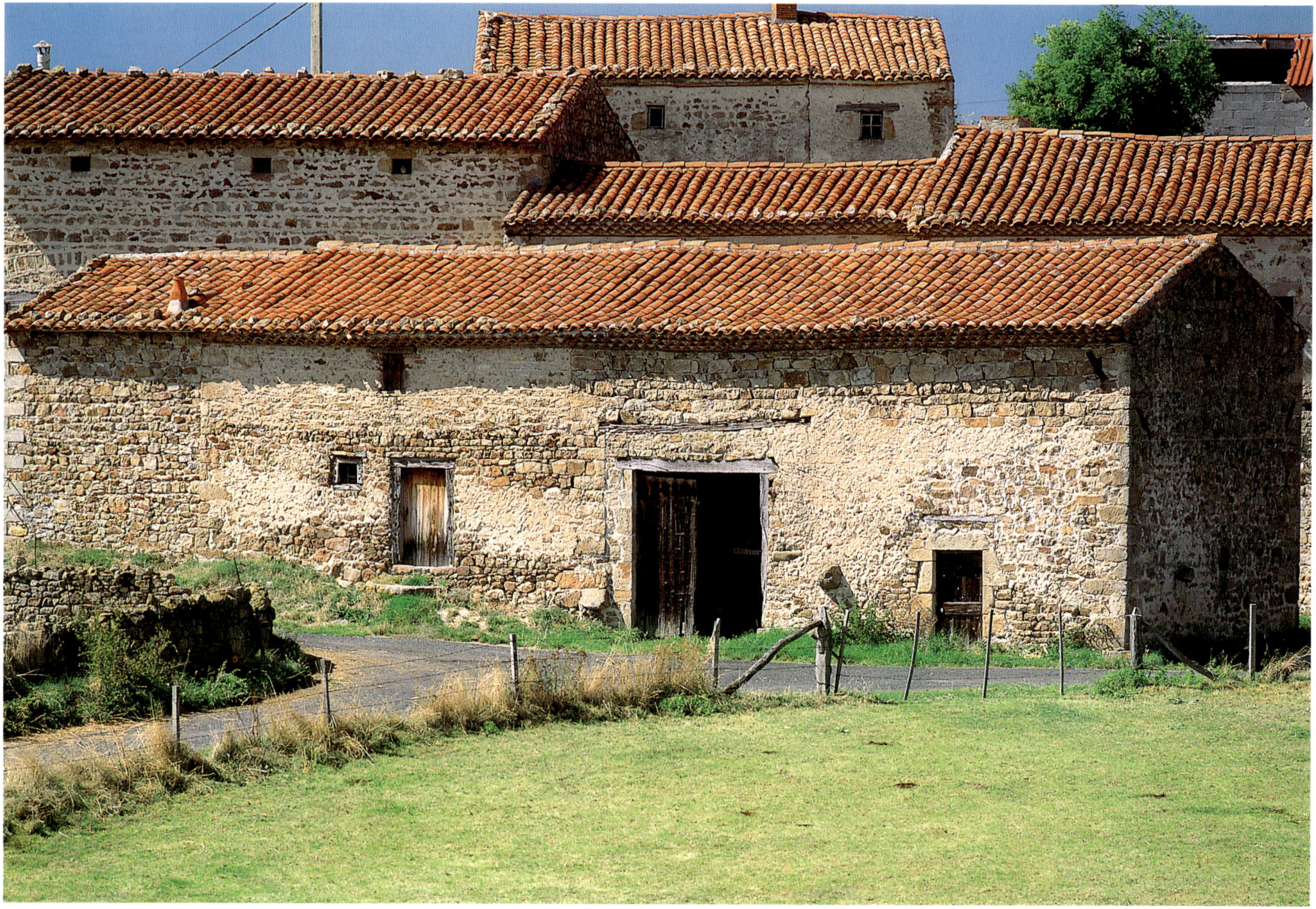

Le Bouchet
Puy-de-Dôme

Light brown granite and orange canal tiles provide a striking colour combination for these farmsteads in the Livradois Forez Regional Park – a gentle pastoral landscape famous for its cheeses. Not so long ago the farmers of this area would take their herds up to the high pasture in the spring. There the women and children would stay on in the 'top farm' called a *jas* or *jasserie*, sleeping on mattresses stuffed with beech leaves and making cheeses. When, however, the women descended with their cheeses at the first sign of winter snow, their menfolk often left the region to work as sawyers or water carriers. The cheeses are given the name of *forme* from the mould they are made in, which is round, measuring 130 mm (5 in) across and 190 mm (7½ in) high. Examples are Forme de Montbrison and Forme de Saint-Anthème but the most famous is the Forme d'Ambert, which is a creamy, old-style, blue-veined cheese and one of thirty French cheeses which have the *appellation d'origine contrôlée*.

Saint-Hostien
Haute-Loire

This lovely building is typical of the Velay region. The living accommodation on the left is arranged on two floors about a central staircase. The nine symmetrically placed openings are a feature of this vernacular style as are the adjoining in-line farm buildings with an upper-level barn reached by an earth ramp, or *montoir*. This type of farmstead is also found in the Saint-Genest-Malifaux region of Pilat to the east. Dark volcanic rocks have been used in the construction and the buildings are beautifully roofed with schist *lauzes*. Note the relieving arches over the dressed stone lintels of the ground-floor windows and the granite cross built into the ridge.

Rudez
Cantal

Grey-blue schist tiles – *lauzes d'Auvergne* – with round edges in a fishscale pattern, cover the steep roofs of these little cottages lying in the shadow of the Monts du Cantal. This solid block of rising crests can be seen from a distance of 200 km (125 miles) away in all directions. Their heights once rose to the peak of a volcano that must have reached 3000 m (10,000 ft) and rivalled Mount Etna since its laval flows covered a circumference of 75 km (45 miles). The limit of this area is today marked by a ring of large towns such as Mauriac, Aurillac and Saint-Flour. Deep valleys radiate from its vanished summit, with their flanks showing black scarps of basalt alternating with solidified lava. At the base of the mountain they broaden out into a fertile land of hedged meadows and orchards growing peaches and even almonds.

Puy Mary
Cantal

This granite-built refuge, once probably a shepherd's hut, is situated on the *Grande Randonnée 4*, one of the great long-distance walking routes that run the length and breadth of France. From this point on the Pas de Peyrol at an altitude of 1589 m (5,214 ft) an easy climb takes you up to the Puy Mary at 1787 m (5,863 ft), which has spectacular views of the nearer valleys separated by narrow ridges. Here the view is northwards up the Impradine valley towards the Monts Dore and the heart of the Volcans D'Auvergne Regional Park.

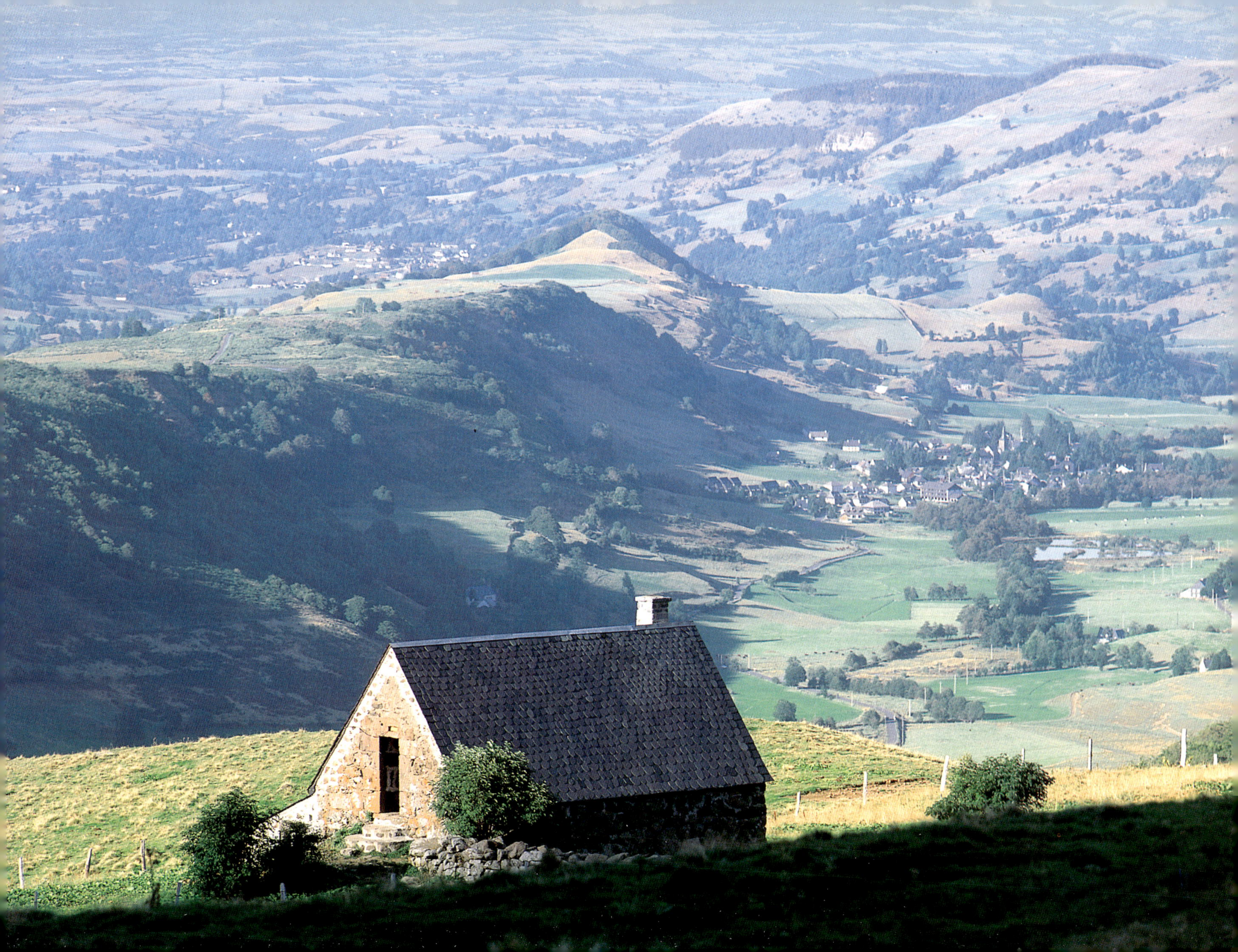

AUVERGNE

Lavigerie
Cantal

In stone-built *bergeries* like this one in the Volcans d'Auvergne Regional Park, shepherds over-wintered and lambed their flocks of sheep. Grass was soon exhausted in the hot dry landscapes of the south. To overcome this problem shepherds drove their sheep from winter pastures in the plains of the Mediterranean and Aquitaine to the summer pastures, or *alpages*, of the Massif Central, the Pyrenees and the Alps. Moving about 20–25 km (12–15 miles) a day under the supervision of specialized shepherds, the flock would journey some 300 km (190 miles). This ancient practice of transhumance carved a pattern of drove roads on the landscape. Sedentary farmers hired out their fields for the transhumant sheep and as a result had their land manured. As Rabelais put it of the sheep of Dindenault, 'in every field where they have pissed, the grain grows as if God himself had pissed on it'.

Murat
Cantal

On the high ground between the deep valleys flowing down from the Monts du Cantal are tablelands called Planaises. The gradual weathering and breaking down of the basalt that covers them makes a stoney but extremely fertile soil, on which cereals will ripen as high as 775 m (2,500 ft). The black basalt stone picked out of it is used to construct field walls as well as farmhouses and farm buildings, like this example with its roof tiles of schist under a semi-circular stone ridge. The highest levels of the Planaises form a mountain area covered in snow for some six months of the year. Their steep sides are forested but the uplands are given over to pasture since the deep basalt soils produce a sweeter grass than the granite. This is where cattle are fattened having been driven some 30 km (20 miles) up the valleys each summer. At one time whole families moved with them taking up residence in wooden chalets called *burons*. Here they make the goat cheese known as Cabecou and the celebrated Cantal cheese.

MIDI-PYRÉNÉES

Saint-Jean-Delnous
Aveyron

A water mill has been on this site for over a thousand years. Much of the present stone-built mill with its *lauzes* roof dates back to mediaeval times, although the crooked door frame is nineteenth century. Until the Revolution it was a feudal dependency of the priory of Ambialet on the Tarn and afterwards remained a working mill up to the end of the Second World War. During the War many water mills were worked unofficially by the miller's wives and children since the millers themselves were either conscripted or deported. Although no longer a working mill, nearly all the machinery is in place, with horizontal (rather than the more usual vertical) drive wheels, three pairs of millstones and a large stone pestle and mortar for making oil (from maize, beechnut or walnut) and cider. The millpond is fed by a millstream led off the main stream, and the flow of water is governed by a clever system of sluice gates and overflows.

Mirandol
Tarn

A simple peasant's dwelling with first-floor living accommodation shows the varied use of the local stone, the versatile schist. Long smooth-sided slabs of it frame the door and window openings and create the treads to the external flight of steps. Split slithers are used as roofing slates with their lower edges making a half-round shape. Stone split to a greater thickness is used to make the voussoirs of the arch above the *cave* entrance while what remains makes sturdy walls.

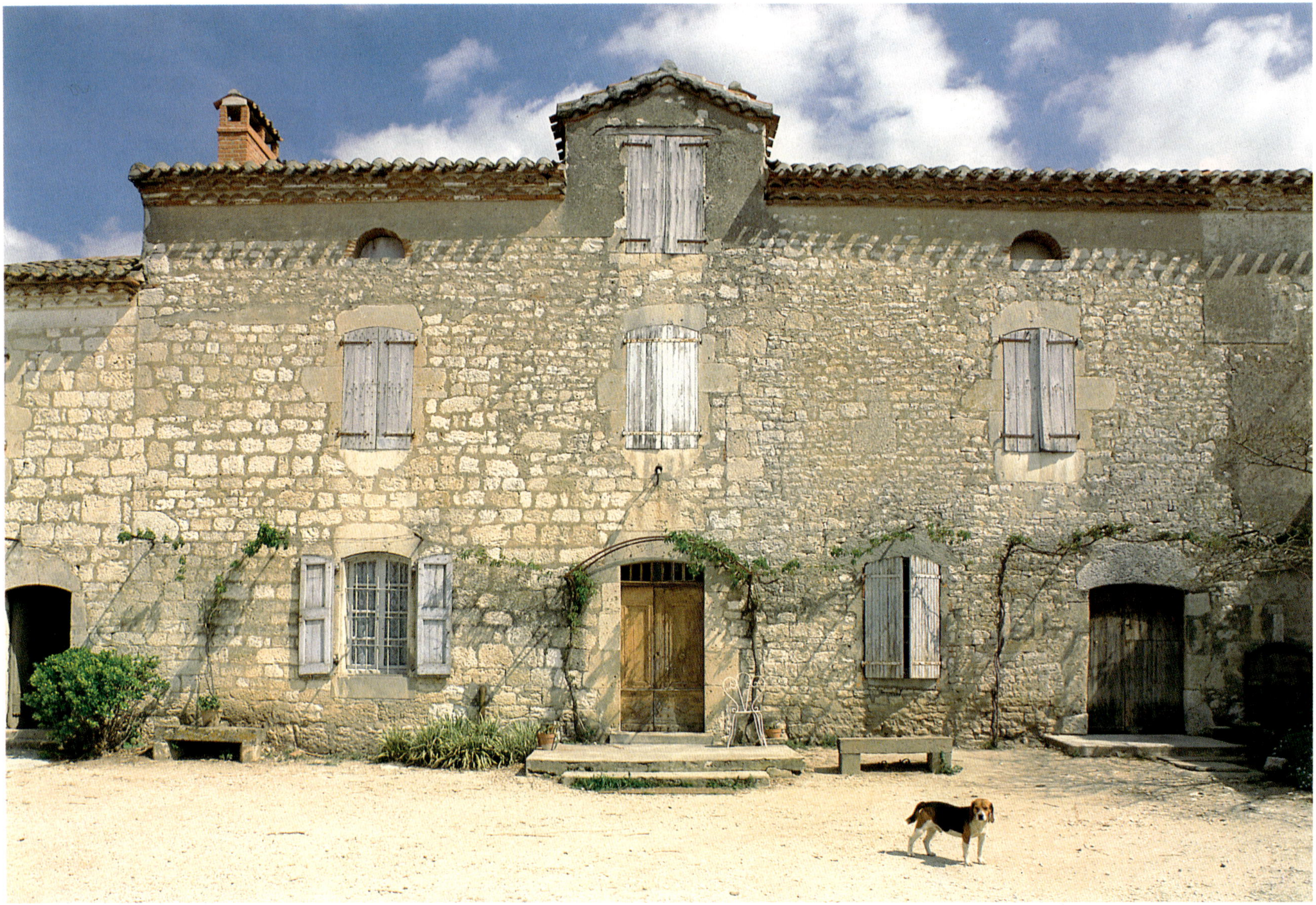

Sainte-Croix
Tarn

This stately and almost symmetrical farmhouse with its flanking buildings is built in cut and coursed limestone blocks, which broadly decrease in size the further they are from the ground. Large, arched stone lintels are used over the doors and windows. Living accommodation is on the ground and first floor while a *grenier* takes up the third floor. Sacks of grain or other items to be stored would be winched into the *grenier* through the centrally placed dormer which has its own pitched roof at right angles to the main roof. Two half-moon-shaped openings provide ventilation. Canal tiles are used as a roof covering throughout. The *génoise*, the series of corbelled canal tiles at the eaves which support the projecting main roof, can be clearly seen. Its name derives from the fact that it was introduced from Genoa by Italian masons in the eighteenth century. Apart from the decorative effect its purpose was to throw rainwater well clear of the walls.

Villefranche-d'Albigeois
Tarn

This open-courtyard farm, situated just south of the River Tarn, lies some 20 km (12 miles) to the east of Albi, called *La Ville Rouge* ('The Red Town') because of its brickwork. Brick is extensively used in the Albigeois, since although the local stone can make a good infill it does not lend itself to substantial or well-dressed corner use. A long building with a single pitch roof is set against a gable end of the farmhouse and provides a link to the courtyard buildings behind. Advantage has been taken of its wall to insert a small dovecot consisting of a triangle of fifteen flight holes. The low-pitched, hipped roof of canal tiles, with its finely detailed *génoise* at the eaves, is a feature of the lowland Albigeois farmhouse.

MIDI-PYRÉNÉES

Escaza
Lot

This farmhouse with its main living quarters on the first floor has great nobility and presence. It shows a form of elevated dwelling found in the south of the region in Quercy, Lot-et-Garonne, Tarn-et-Garonne and in the neighbouring *département* of Tarn. A wide, generously proportioned flight of stone steps rises above the cowshed and the cellar or sheep-pens to an open varandah called a *bolet*, whose roof is carried on turned stone columns with broad spreading capitals. Here the family could gather to work, chat and look out over their land and that of their neighbour's while sheltered from the sun and the rain. From this verandah you gain access not only to the living rooms but also to a tall, elegant tower and *pigeonnier*, which dominates the surrounding countryside. The height of this tower is exaggerated by the steeply pitched roof and extended even further by the two decorative ridge finials. Pigeons gain acess through openings, including nine flight holes cut in one limestone block, set above a ledge towards the top of the tower.

Fontanes
Lot

Mushroom-shaped limestone staddles prevent rats entering this fine free-standing dovecot framed by acacia trees. The dovecot itself is a timber-framed construction infilled with clay tiles laid either horizontally or in chevron patterns. There is a timber landing platform to the flight holes above the door but birds may also be able to fly in and out under the eaves of the four-sided lantern roof, with its elegant finial. Flat clay tiles are used throughout but with half-round canal tiles for the ridges.

Béon
Pyrénées-Atlantiques

This 'L'-shaped village farm lies beside the Gave d'Ossau (*gave* being local dialect for 'torrent') in the Vallée d'Ossau. A wing of farm buildings is set at right-angles to the farmhouse with its living accommodation placed over the ground floor *cave*. A slate tile roof encloses walls made up of the stone detritus brought down by the *gave*, liberally mixed with a lime mortar. It is an area of scattered farms and hamlets, small cereal fields, irrigated meadows, gardens and orchards, where flocks of sheep and herds of cattle browse the upper pastures all summer long. This deep valley separates the western Pyrenees, with its lush forests of oak and ash, high rainfall and mild winters, from the central Pyrenees with its alpine-like massif, wild gorges and year-round snow. This in turn is quite distinct from the eastern Pyrenees bordering the Mediterranean with its clear blue skies, hot summer days, evergreen oaks and olive groves.

Bages
Pyrénées-Atlantiques

Four slabs of slate make a ventilation slit in the gable end of a simple mountain hut in the valley of the Ossau. Slate is easy to find and use in this valley, which rises steeply to the French Pyrénées Occidentales National Park and the Spanish National Park of Ordesa. These national parks provide the last refuge of the Pyrenean bear, of which there are only about thirty still in existence. They are also the home for large herds of isard (Pyrenean mountain goats, the French park's symbol) and for Egyptian, griffon and bearded vultures.

AQUITAINE

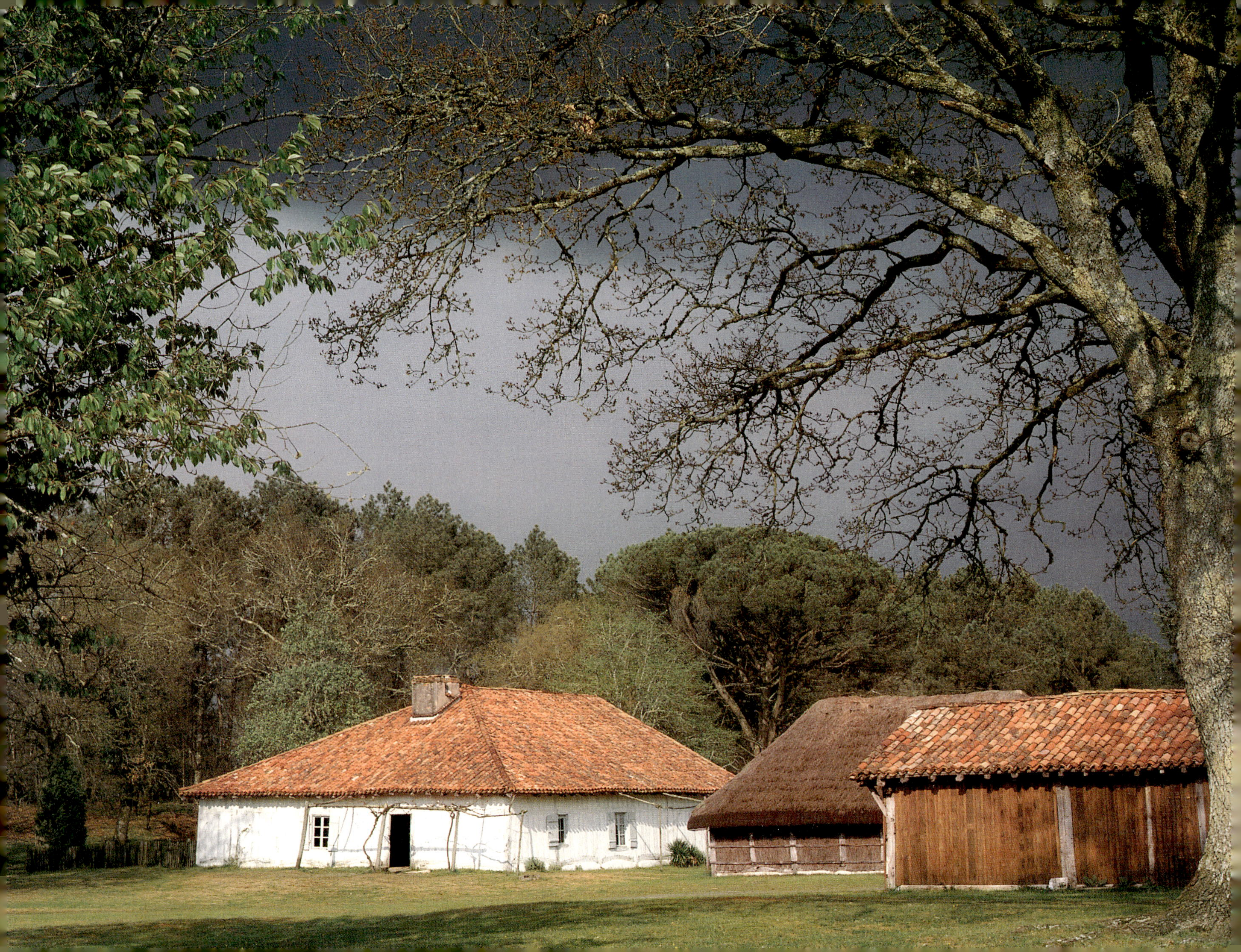

Marquèze
Landes

The red and white farm buildings of the Landes, like these at Marquèze Ecomusée, make simple yet powerful statements amid pastures seemingly carved out of forests of oak and predominantly pine. No part of Aquitaine is so completely dominated by the Atlantic as is the Landes. The winds blowing in strongly from the sea have spread fine sand over a coastal area of 300 km (190 miles) in length. For centuries it was nothing but a desert, but in the eighteenth century Bremontier discovered that hurdle fencing, the planting of marram grass and (once these had anchored the sand) belts of pine trees would bring about the greening of the desert. Now, behind the great 100 m (350 ft)-high coastal dunes lies a free flowing forest of pine trees, from whose trunks resin is often collected in little wooden beakers, hung below a long, shallow groove cut into the bark. The marshes that shepherds once strode through on stilts are now drained to form meadows for the raising of stock.

Marquèze
Landes

The farmhouses of the Landes are nearly square in shape and covered by a broad-spreading, ground-hugging, three-sided roof clad with canal tiles. They are orientated east-west with a hip on the western end to protect this façade from the wind and weather coming off the sea. This allows the centre section of the eastern elevation, called the *eustandade*, to be completely open to the warmth of the morning sun, like this façade of the house of a farmer and landlord, the back of which is visible in the photograph opposite. Whitened with lime, a flurry of oak posts and pine beams and braces create a lattice wall in front of an open area where the family can sit sheltered from wind, rain and overhead sun alike. This graceful display of woodwork is itself protected by an *auvent* – a projection of the roof carried on cantilevered purlins, or beams.

Marquèze
Landes

This elevated *poulailler*, or henhouse, in the Écomusée is solidly constructed in riven timber and capped with canal tiles. A notched pole permits the hens to climb up to a safe night roost without allowing their predators, including the resourceful fox, to follow. Originally the French for fox was *goupil* but it changed to *renard* after the name of the fox character in the mediaeval stories about the cockerel Chanticleer. Height also protects the local black-or grey-plummaged hens from ground humidity and keeps them clean, since the slatted floor allows droppings to fall to the ground, where they can be collected to fertilize the acid soil of the kitchen gardens. From these chicken coops in the first light of morning hens launch themselves, in squawking balls of feathers, to hit the ground running.

Villandraut
Gironde

A carved truss extends across the width of the eastern façade of this landowner's house in the Landes. It carries the roof forward to provide a sitting-out area at ground level and covering for a first-floor balcony with an ornate balustrade supported by posts. The Landes – the extensive drainage basin of the River Leyre – was divided into parcels of land called *quartiers*, whose inhabitants comprised landlords, *métayers* and *brassiers*. *Métayers* were tenant farmers, or sharecroppers, who paid the landlord half of their rye harvest and a third of any other grain and vegetables they produced, together with some poultry, eggs and cuts of pork. A *brassier* (from *bras* meaning 'arm') was a simple agricultural worker, who literally only had his arms to hire out.

AQUITAINE

Parranquet
Lot-et-Garonne

This tight-knit complex of farmhouse and farm buildings displays an interesting array of typically Perigordian roofs. The far farmhouse with its freshly rendered chimney has a four-sided mansard roof, which provides more habitable roof space. In Périgord the traditional canal tile is often used on the shallow upper pitch but the lower pitch is too steep for anything other than flat clay tiles, which can be nailed to cross-battens. Here with comparatively steep pitches flat tiles have been used throughout. The square *pigeonnier* in front of it has a four-sided roof, which like the mansard roof flattens out over the eaves in a delightful curve called a *coyau*. This takes rainwater well clear of the walls in conjunction with the supporting *génoise* corbelling (just visible) under the eaves. The roof of the timber-fronted tobacco drying barn in the foreground and the roof to the left have the more prevalent, shallow, double-pitched roofs covered in canal tiles, which are also used throughout as hip and ridge tiles.

L'Héritier
Lot-et-Garonne

A certain grandeur sets this farmstead apart and perhaps indicates a close association with the nearby Château Biron. For one thing the living quarters are arranged on the first floor and entered by a covered terrace or gallery, which is unusual for this part of Périgord. For another there is the great round-arched entrance to the ground-floor *cave*. But most telling of all is the remarkably large, circular *pigeonnier*. It reminds us that dovecots were more than functional, they were also status symbols. Sizeable dovecots were restricted to large landowners, even in the south which was more liberal than the north in this respect, because birds would feed on standing crops over a wide area of countryside. Consequently, to build a *pigeonnier* housing as many birds as this required the large landholding of a powerful landowner to accommodate them. Its internal walls are punctured by row upon row of nests, which are reached by a ladder on an arm projecting from a central pivoting post called a *potence* – a medieval French invention.

AQUITAINE

AQUITAINE

Beynac
Dordogne

This honey-coloured *pigeonnier* is roofed in limestone *lauzes*, which have been used to convert a square plan at the eaves into a domed roof crowned by the traditional finial. This roof and its large dormers, providing access for the birds, make it unusual even in a part of France exceedingly rich in *pigeonniers*. The Romans kept pigeons in a *columbarium* or *peristeron*, which could hold as many as 5000 birds, and probably introduced the dovecot to France. Certainly they set down the five basic requirements for keeping pigeons – ease of access, shelter, nesting facilities, ventilation and protection from vermin – which have remained the same ever since.

Le Pic
Dordogne

Soft white limestone, pale yellow render, steep tile-encrusted hipped roofs and a shallow-pitched lean-to combine to make a very traditional group of farm buildings, tightly gathered about a small courtyard. The hipped roofs flair at the eaves in an overhang carried on a two-row, canal-tile *génoise*, while at the ridge of the higher farmhouse two terracotta finials mark the junction between the ridge tiles and the hip tiles.

Issigeac
Dordogne

A tributary of the River Dropt runs past the limestone walls of this sixteenth- to seventeenth-century courtyarded farmstead and former magistrate's house in Périgord Noir. A bridge across the stream leads through a *porte cochère* to the courtyard. From there a short flight of stone steps leads up to a *bolet*, an open-air porch fronting the entrance to the first-floor living accommodation. The *bolet* is given a fanciful ogee, or onion-dome roof covered in fishscale-shaped *ardoise de pays* slates. The central section of the farmhouse has a mansard roof with a shallow upper pitch covered in canal tiles and is flanked by two wings with steep, hipped roofs using flat tiles. Timber beams on curved, stone corbels carry a small corner tower and pigeon loft.

Monbazillac
Dordogne

When you see vines almost entering the front door of a house and a marked reluctance to allow land to be used for any other purpose than the making of wine or the growing of grapes, you can be reasonably sure it is the house of a *vigneron*, a wine producer. Although the accommodation here is all on the ground floor, this is a spacious and elegant house, well-endowed with fireplaces and tall, gracious windows under delicately curved limestone lintels. The double-pitch mansard roof with flat tiles on the lower, steep pitch and canal tiles on the upper, shallow pitch creates a more useful loft space. It is lit and ventilated by triangular openings called *outeaux*, which with timber frames carved in the form of a trefoil are a typically Perigordian feature. These vines produce the white grapes used to make Monbazillac, the leading sweet wine of the Bergerac region.

AQUITAINE

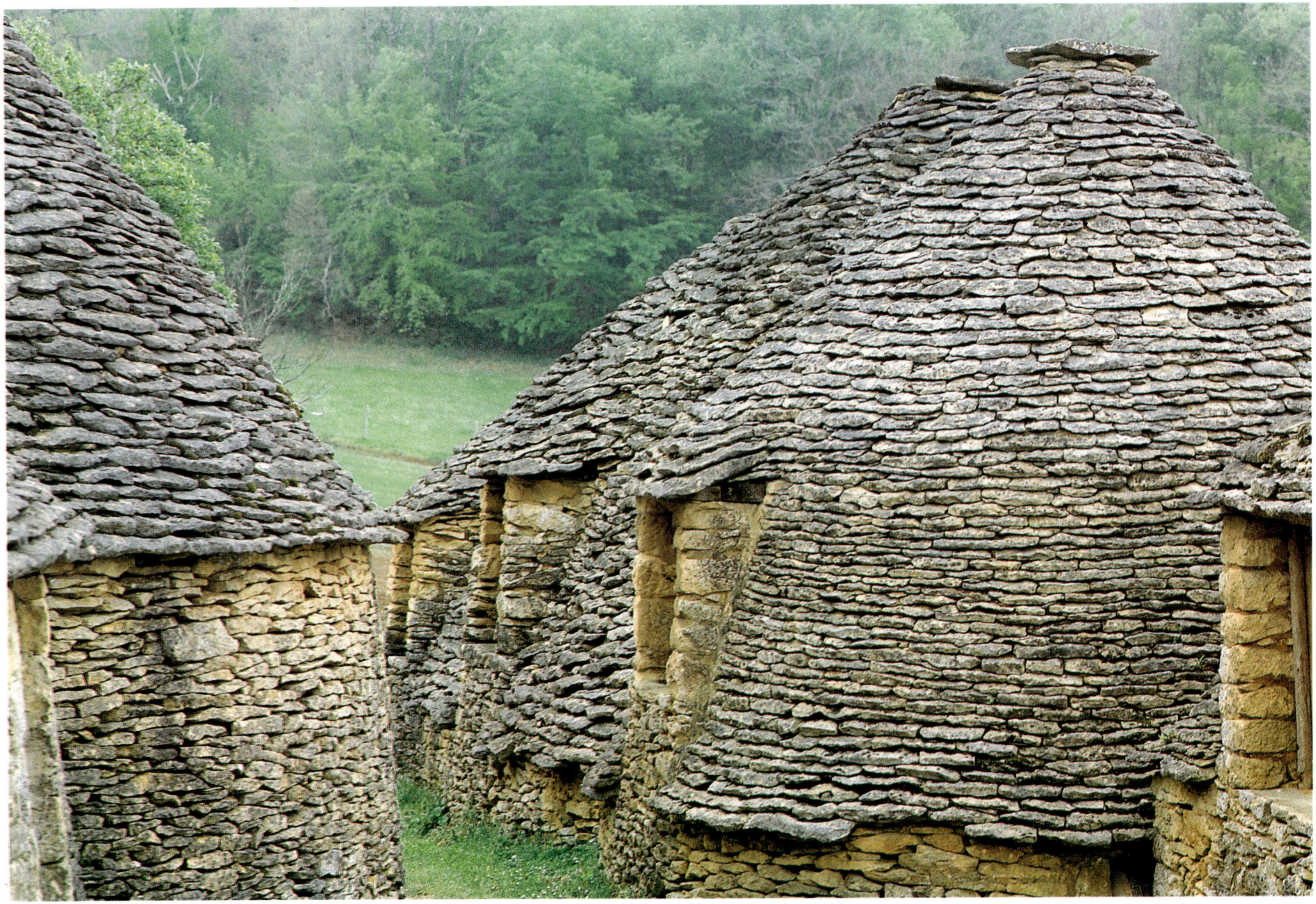

Sireuil
Dordogne

Called *caselles* in Quercy, *jasseries* in the Causses, *bories* in Provence and *cadolles* in Burgundy, these extraordinary dry-stone buildings are known as *garriottes* here in Périgord Noir. There are ten of them in this farmstead comprising a farmhouse and farm buildings, which are mostly interconnecting. They are built without mortar and with a minimum of timber roof structure, if any at all, simply using limestone picked off the fields by a process called *épierrement*. The collected stone is sorted and left in piles to weather in the open air. The best stones are then used as building material with the fatter being employed in the walls and the thinner on the roof. The roofs are constructed at a steep 53° to 58° angle so that the weight of the heavy stone tiles is transferred more to the outside wall than to the slender timber roof framework. This pitch also allows the tiles to be laid almost horizontally with each cantilevering inwards slightly beyond the one underneath to create the beehive-shaped vault of the farm buildings. A large, flat slab of stone caps the apex of the roof.

Les Eyzies-de-Tayac
Dordogne

Wisteria covers a cottage built into a limestone *abri*, or rock shelter. People have always used these overhangs in the deep valley of the Vézère since Cro-Magnon man sheltered in them and decorated their walls 30,000 years ago. All in all there are 25 caves and 100 sites in the valley with marks of early man which range from the polychrome painting in the Font de Gaume to France's most important collection of rock engravings in the Combarelles Cave. The most famous are the Lascaux Caves discovered in 1940 with their 1500 drawings and paintings. However, the fungal bloom caused by people and air made it necessary to close the caves some twenty years ago. Remarkably a complete facsimile – Lascaux II – was then created nearby over the next ten years, including every nook and cranny of the original.

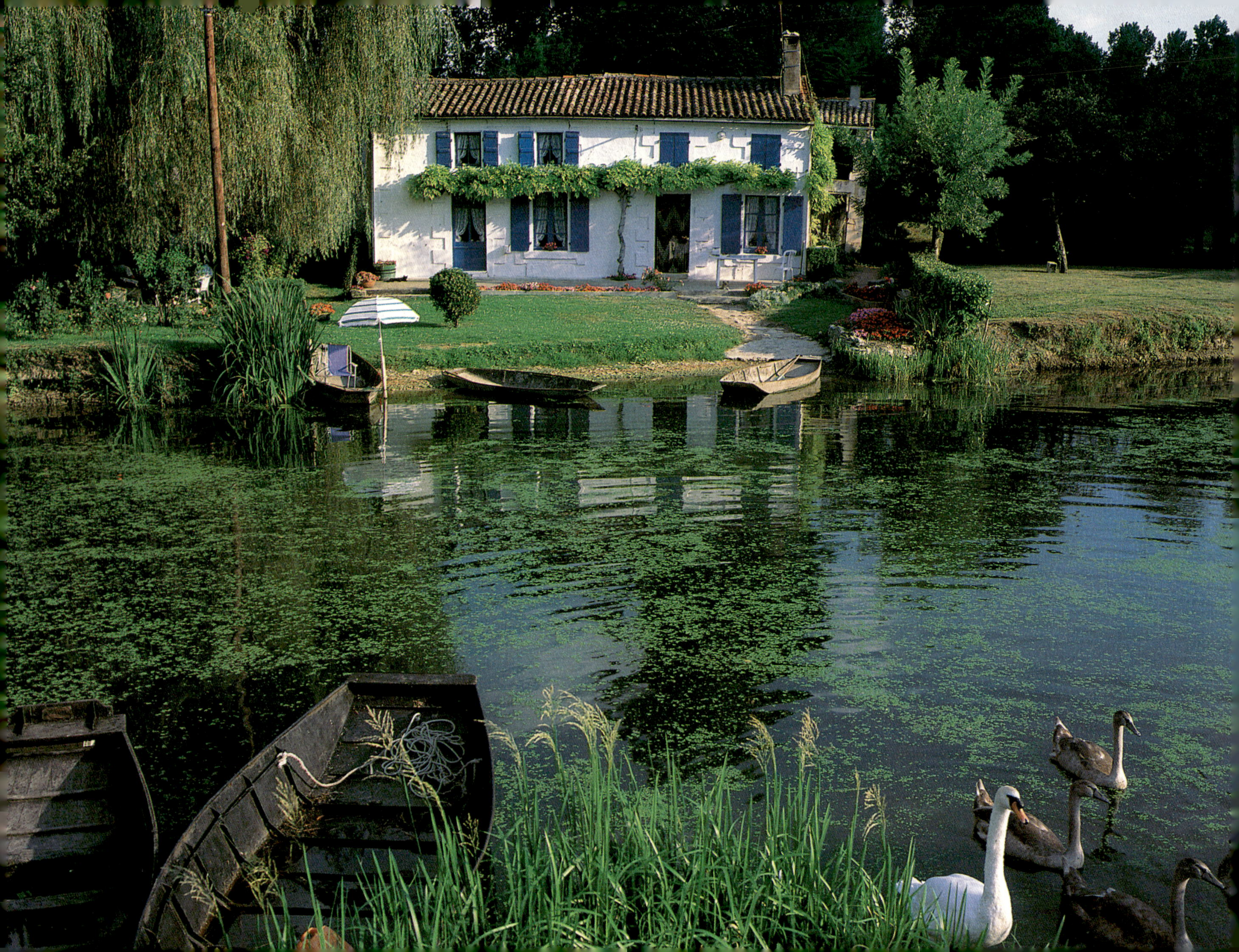

Coulon
Deux Sèvres

When the River Sèvre Niortaise silted up its exit to the sea, it created a marshland, the Marais Poitevin (now a regional park), which flooded in winter. However, from the Middle Ages onwards the monks of the local abbey slowly drained the area by means of a network of little canals called *les conches*. Today there is a distinct division between a dry, arable and treeless area in the west and a wet area in the east. Coulon, a former sailors' village, lies in the wet area called La Venise Verte, 'Green Venice'. At the beginning of the nineteenth century water covered the wet area for eight months of the year, so you could not grow anything and all movement had to be by boat. The inhabitants lived by hunting, fishing and exploiting the willow, ash, poplar and alders, which tolerated these wet conditions. The people came to be known as *huttiers* from the primitive dwellings they originally lived in, but with greater prosperity they built two-storey stone houses called *cabanes*, like this one on the banks of the Sèvre.

Coulon
Deux Sèvres

This *cabane* in the Marais Mouillé, the wet area of the Marais Poitevin, can only be reached by boat along the River Sèvre Niortaise, which it borders, and the network of small canals known as *les conches*. Built after 1830, it is constructed in stone bound with a clay mortar and only rendered with a whitewashed lime mortar on the northern façade seen here facing the river. In these conditions the *cabanes* are built on a raft of stone, since standard foundation footings would have produced an unstable building. The roof covering is of canal tiles with clipped eaves and a gutter. The farmhouse dwelling, with lofts above, is linked by an internal door to a cowshed on the left (behind the willow), with a characteristically open hay loft above, maximizing cross-draft ventilation in this damp climate. External woodwork was traditionally painted in light green, pale blue or *en Bordeaux* – claret red.

La Garette
Deux Sèvres

The shutters and doors of this simple-looking, limestone-built and lime-washed *cabane* in the Marais Poitevin are painted in the traditional pale blue. But the simplicity is misleading since from this roadside façade the land falls sharply to a canal, and the farmhouse and its adjoining farm building run across the slope to give a long side elevation and a tall three-storey waterside barn. A shallow asymmetrical pitch of local canal tiles in rose and ochre covers this long, substantial farmhouse, and the barn has an upper level open to the drying winds with its roof carried on limestone pillars. All transport, of hay, reeds, wood, crops and animals, would have been along the canal.

Vouillé
Vienne

This cheerful and well-appointed cottage stands in one of the sunniest regions of France with over 2,000 hours of sunshine per annum. It seems content and at peace in its kitchen garden even though the mad rush of twentieth-century agribusiness comes very close to its gable end. These gables exposed to the prevailing winds are built with the best stone gathered from nearby fields. By contrast the main façade facing south-east and the rear facing north-west are built with a rendered mixture of poorer-quality stone – *tout-venant* – and clay. The sharp-edged quoins and surrounds to the door and window openings are made of lime mortar shaped to look like stone. Tall chimneys gracing each gable wall and a canal-tile roof carried well beyond the eaves to protect the walls complete the picture.

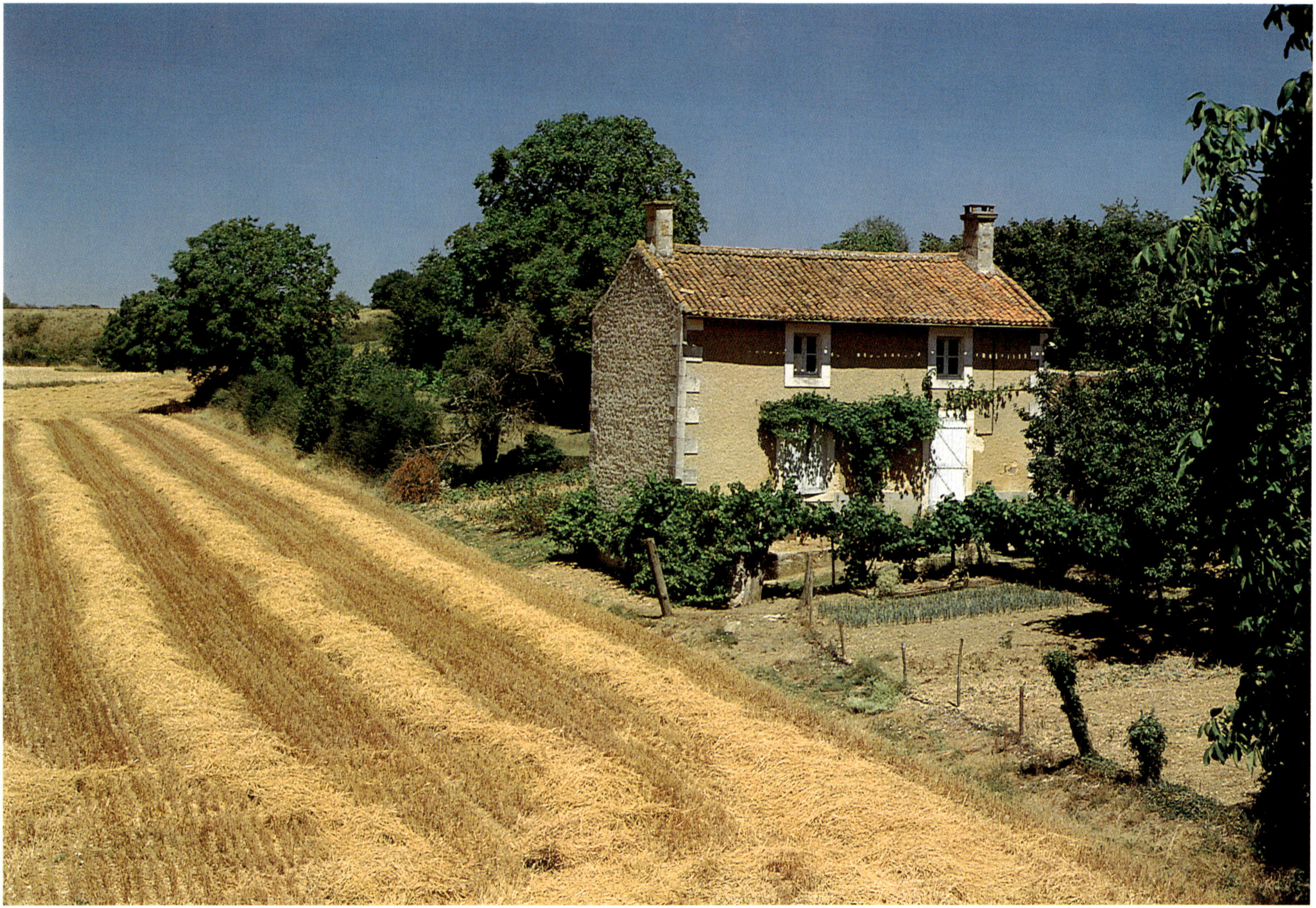

Île de Fedrun
Loire-Atlantique

The Brière is a marshy depression of 7000 hectares (270 square miles) just to the north of St Nazaire at the mouth of the River Loire. On 8 August 1462 Francois II, Duke of Brittany, granted Brière to the twenty-one villages, Fedrun being among them, which mostly occupy islands of higher land in the marshes. These island villages are surrounded by a circular canal called the *curée*. The centre of the island is occupied by uncultivated common land defined by a ring road running right round the island. The village houses are built at right angles to this road and between it and the *curée*, with their gardens called *courtils* running down to the canal. Here are moored the small black punts, called *chalands*, and the larger punts for carrying crops, peat and livestock, called *blins*, which were the main means of transport. The ordered layout of these villages, reinforced by the repetitive use of the standard, whitewashed, stone and thatched-roof cottage known as *la chaumière briéronne*, stands in marked contrast to the surrounding wilderness of reed beds.

Kerhinet
Loire-Atlantique

A notable characteristic of the *chaumière briéronne* is the sparse use of windows. This is explained by the window tax which existed before the French Revolution and resulted in the openings rarely consisting of more than a door, a ground-floor window beside it and a small window to the loft above, which pushed up the eaves line of the thatch in a raised eyebrow or bicorn hat shape. Thatch made from reed, which was cut from November onwards and left in stooks to dry, was used throughout the Brière on steep 50° pitches to a thickness of 1 m (3 ft 3 in) or more. The ridge was usually protected by a capping of puddled clay, but unlike the clay caps to the thatched cottages of Brotonne on the mouth of the Seine in Normandy, no flowers were planted in it.

PAYS DE LA LOIRE

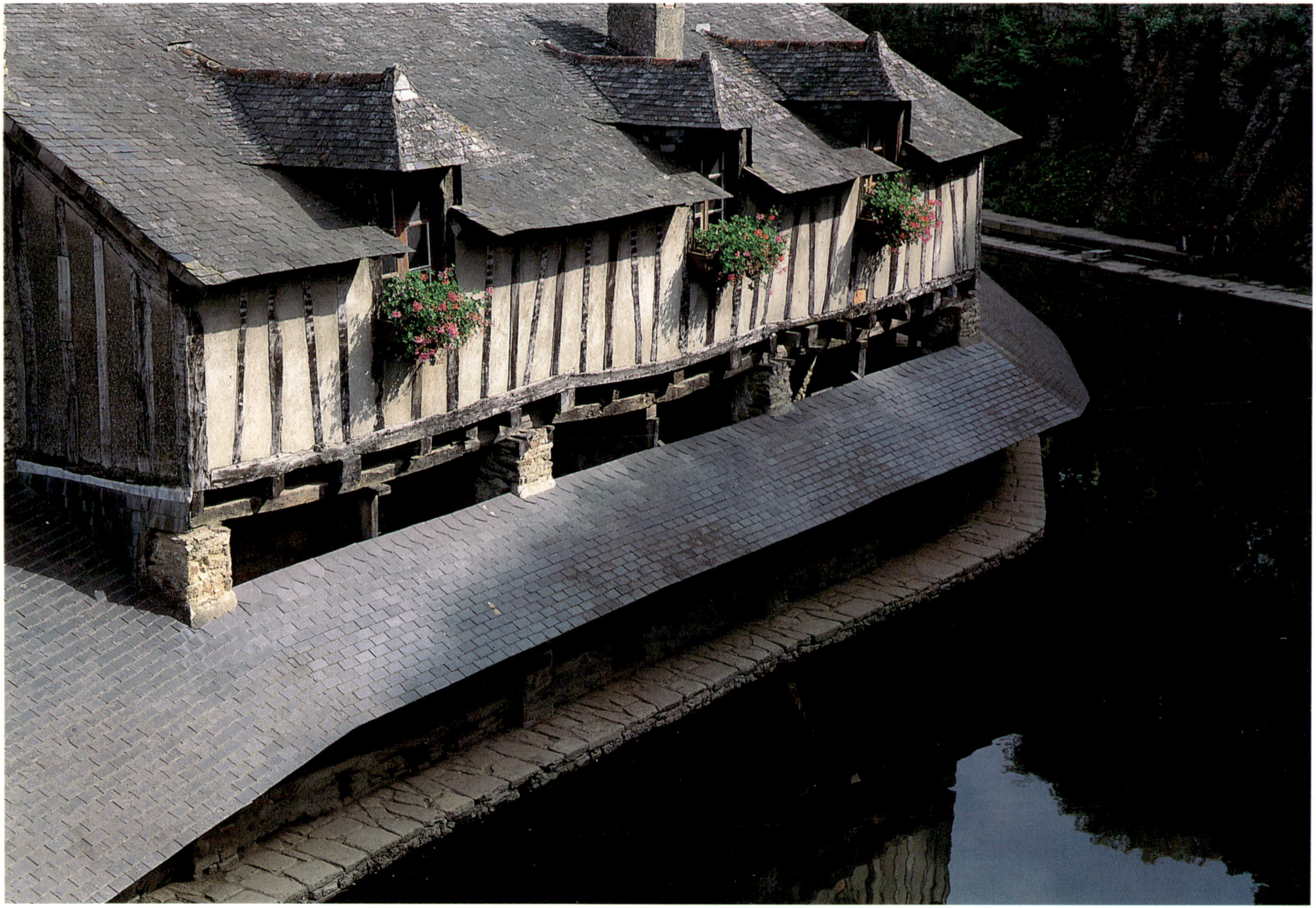

Vannes
Morbihan

These public wash-houses beside the Rohan brook date from the seventeenth century. Locally known as *doues* but generally called *lavoirs*, they were one of the great communal meeting places of France and remained very much in use until some fifteen years ago. To the noisy accompaniment of women gossiping and children playing, clothes were beaten, rubbed, slapped and squeezed on slabs of stone sloping inwards to large rectangular or square troughs of running water. As these were important and prominent buildings they were frequently used for a display of architecture and civic pride. Here stone pillars carry the slate roof over the wash houses, leaving the sides open, and continue upwards to support the timber-framed building above. The finely detailed dormer windows called *lucarnes* are covered with individual hipped roofs, which advance protectively over the windows below. This particular style of roof on a dormer window is called *à la capucine* because it resembles the hood of a Capuchin monk.

Kerberon
Morbihan

This detail shows part of a longhouse on the River Blavet in Vannetais, built of granite and schist originally under a thatched roof. It was restored in 1863, though probably using dressed stone of a much earlier date. The door on the right with its carved stone lintel leads into the all-purpose communal room – kitchen, living room and bedroom – while a door on the left of the steps (not visible) is the entrance to the cowshed. An internal door leads directly from the communal room to the cowshed. The stone steps lead up to a first-floor hay loft. The space under the steps was usefully employed to provide the dog with a home as good, if not better than, that of its master. The longhouse continues to the right of the picture to provide a further family with a single-room dwelling and an adjoining cellar.

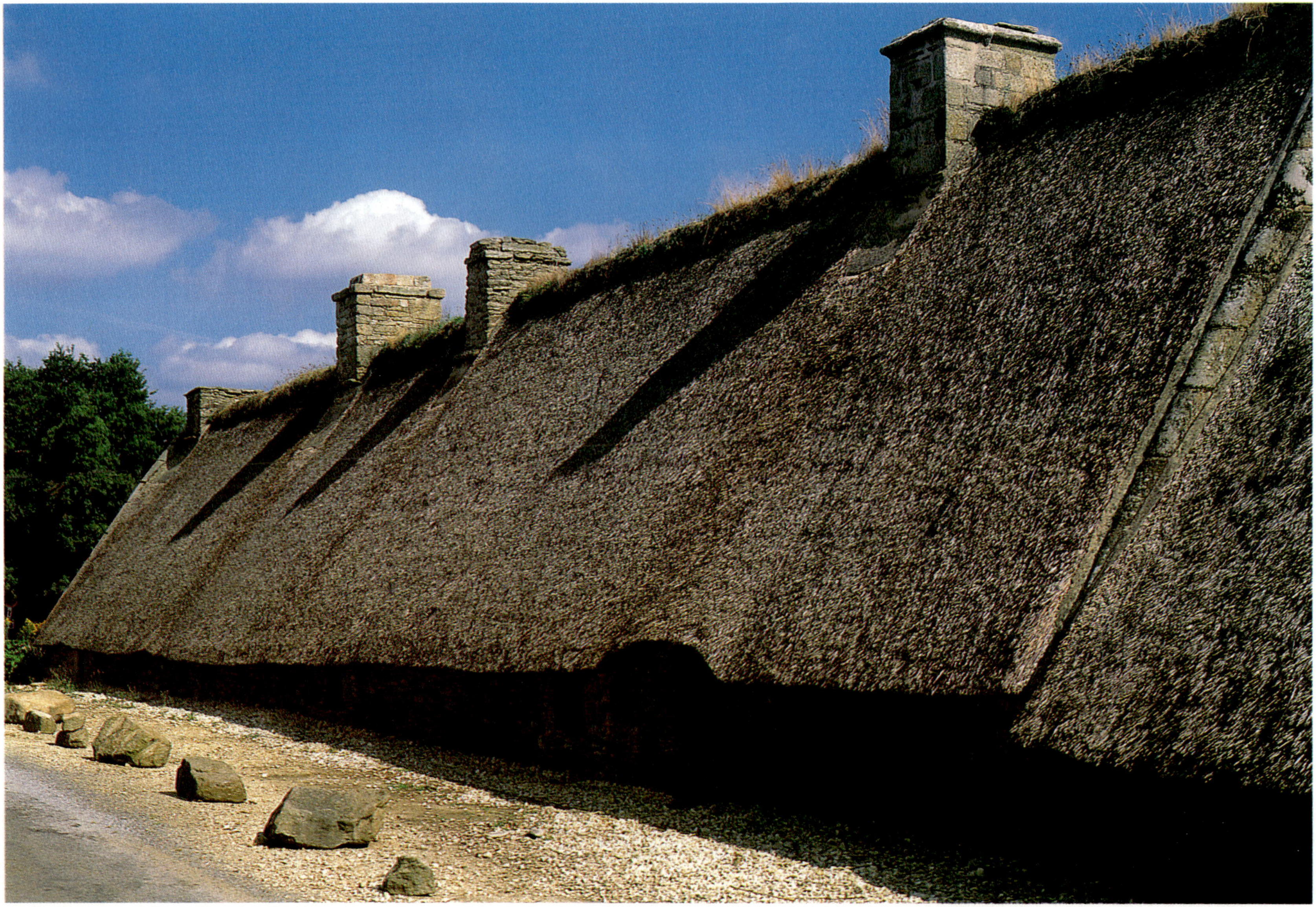

Poul-Fetan
Morbihan

A reed-thatched Breton longhouse, with its living and animal accommodation in one long building, is set into a bank to shelter it from the prevailing south-westerly winds. There are few large towns in this largely agricultural and densely populated region. Its people have always lived either in isolated farmsteads or in hamlets. In the hamlets it is not uncommon to find rows of farms called *rangées* or *rangs*, made up of as many as a dozen such longhouses standing in lines. The countryside about them was, until recent agrarian reforms and the *remembrement* (amalgamation and rationalization of land holdings), a patchwork landscape called *bocage*, which was made up of small, often minute, narrow fields enclosed by stone walls or earthen banks, sometimes with stone revetments. These were planted with shrubs and trees, mostly oak, which acted as windbreaks and provided firewood through pollarding and coppicing. A dense network of lanes, often sunken, thread through the *bocage* in directions dictated by the medieval division of fields and property.

Meriadec
Morbihan

The granite walls of this simple labourer's cottage are flecked with orange-coloured lichen and enveloped in a thick thatch roof. The windows are invariably positioned in the south- or south-east-facing façade to light the ground-floor living room and to light and ventilate the first-floor loft. The way chosen to accommodate this upper opening is always by simply lifting the thatch in a graceful oval curve over the window. However, this approach limits the number of loft openings to one in 7 m (23 ft) of roof line, two in 7–11 m (23–36 ft) or three in more than 15 m (49 ft). The preferred means of giving the thatch a waterproof ridge in this part of Brittany is by a thick capping of lime mortar – *mortier de chaux grasse* – of one-third slaked lime to two-thirds sand.

Kérouat
Finistère

Hard, granite walls covered with ochre-coloured lichen, a fine rounded door-arch in cut stone and roofs of slate in diminishing courses adorn this group of buildings known collectively as the Moulins de Kérouat, the mills of Kérouat. They comprise the houses, mills, bread oven and washing pool of a village of millers built between the seventeenth and twentieth centuries in the Montagnes d'Arrée. The village is now preserved by the Armorique Regional Park.

Gouarec
Côtes-du-Nord

The sober, near-black local slate of this area can be cleaved into flat-sided slabs ideal for building. Sorted according to thickness, they can be used to construct a coursed and finely jointed cottage, like this eighteenth-century example, which is well able to resist the onslaught of wind and rain. The large slabs used as lintels and surrounds to the openings are usually left smooth-faced. However, they can be decoratively carved as can be seen on the cornice and half-round, banded cap on the *lucarne* (dormer window) with its central fleur-de-lis. Finely split slates are also used on the roof, with large slates at the eaves diminishing to small slates at the ridge. The saw-tooth slate ridge is a characteristic feature in Brittany. Also typical is the little shrine to the Virgin Mary – la Sainte Vierge – built into the wall to place the cottage under her protection.

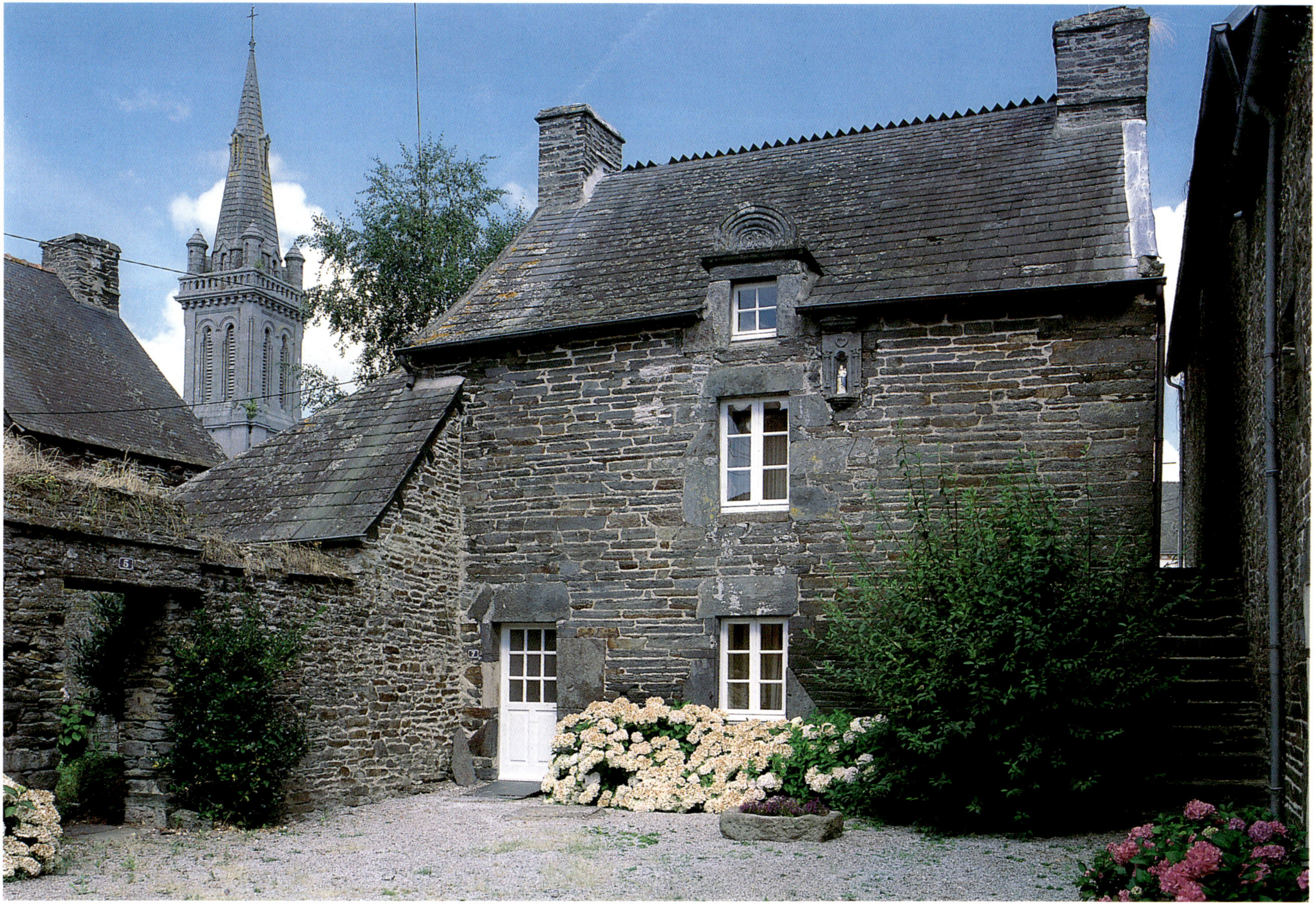

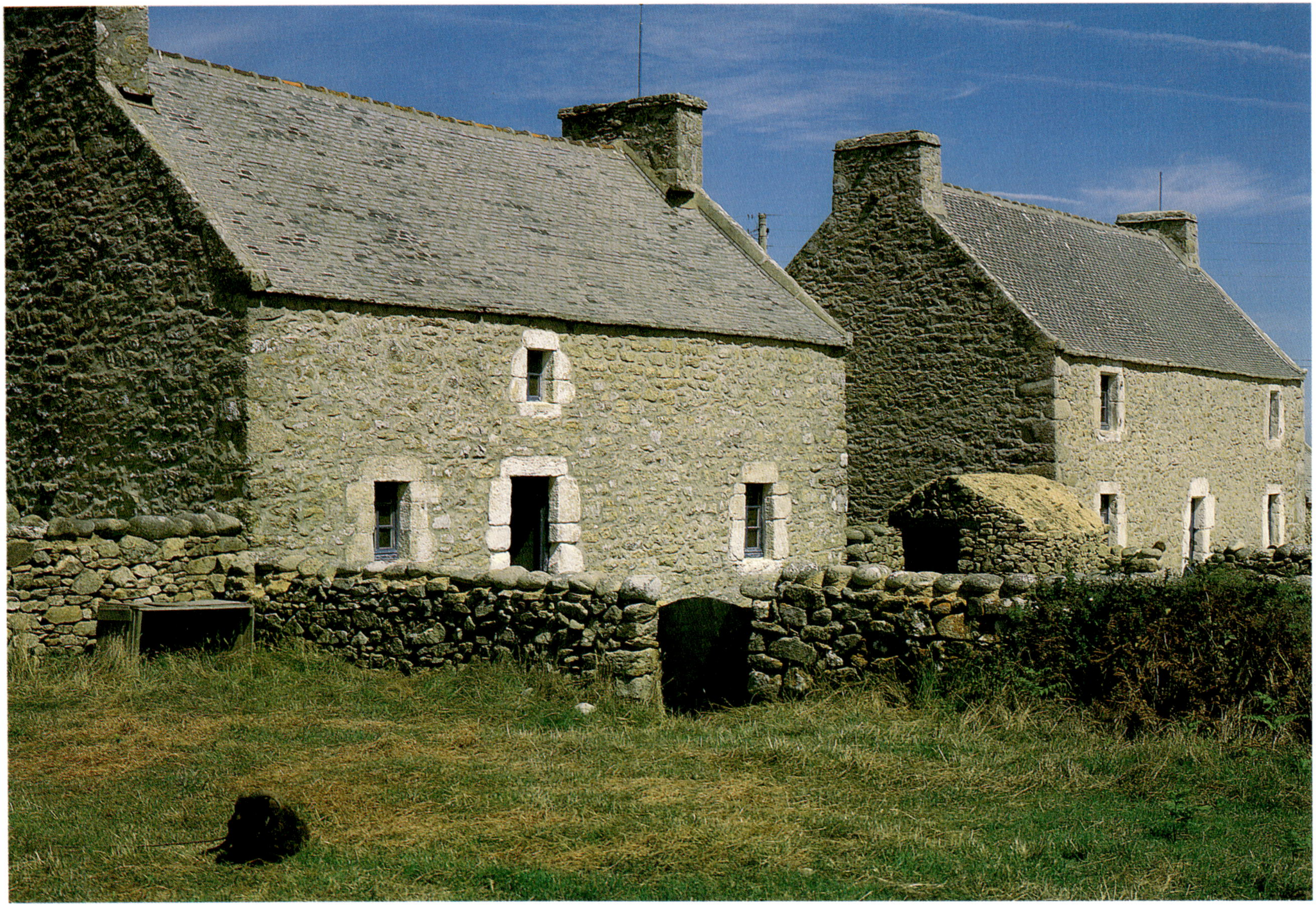

Île d'Ouessant
Finistère

Called Ushant by the sea-faring English who could not pronounce the French word, these windswept, treeless islands in the Iroise Sea lie surrounded by reefs and strong currents some 20 km (12 miles) off the western part of Brittany. The men of the islands spent the greater part of their lives at sea and were frequently lost at sea. Consequently there developed a well-knit society of women, who worked the land, tended the sheep, weaved, made clothes, built the houses, brought up the families and prayed in front of the Proella cross – an effigy of the husband or son missing at sea. The architecture of granite, with roof slates bedded down in mortar against the frequent gales – as shown in this example (now an *écomusée*) – is austere and in marked contrast to the brightly coloured interiors. There were no internal walls: the two ground-floor rooms – a kitchen and a parlour called the *penn brau* (the 'pretty room') – were separated by a wall of furniture made from shipwreck timber washed up on the shore and gaily painted to disguise its imperfections.

Île d'Ouessant
Finistère

Even the smallest cottager with a small sheltered garden, a little land and one or two sheep could prosper by sharing the large communal grazing areas that covered the island. For much of the year (February to September) the sheep were kept in paddocks about the house, where they were attached to long tethers to control grazing, but for the rest of the year they roamed the island. This not only solved the problem of winter feeding but also ensured the production of lambs if you only had ewes, since they would be running with the rams during the October-November tupping period. At the beginning of February a festival marked the gathering of the sheep from off the salt marshes by the whole community. Each family claimed its own sheep by ear markings and paid a due, currently 12 francs, on each animal.

Runan
Côtes-du-Nord

This type of simple dwelling lived in by Breton fishermen or labourers is called a *pentwin* or *penty*. It is solidly built in cut and coursed stone but the accommodation is the usual basic two rooms on the ground floor with a storage loft above. The slate roof is raised to cover the small door through which goods are taken into the loft in the roof space. Bedrooms were unusual and instead *lits clos* – covered and curtained beds (also found in the Queyras region of Savoy) – were ranged along the wall of the living room. The owner, seen here struggling into the customary blue working jacket as he leaves his house, is wearing wooden *sabots*, or clogs. These are rarely seen now but once everyone, even fishermen (whose clogs were made out of the better-gripping alder), wore them, and each village had at least one *sabotier*, or clog-maker.

Plougrescant
Côtes-du-Nord

Brittany is the peninsular part of the Armorican massif, a series of parallel east-west orientated belts of primary strata, largely comprising granites, sandstones and schists. The sea drives into these long slithers of rock on three sides creating a ragged, shredded coastline 1200 km (750 miles) long. Here the primary stratum is a rose pink granite, which gives its name to the coast, the Côte de Granit Rosé. The steady erosion by salt, sea, wind and frost have left crinkled outcrops of granite, which have here been used to provide both shelter and building material for a fisherman's *penty*. It turns its back on the south-west sea winds and opens up to the warmth and sun of the south-east.

BRITTANY

Beaumont-sur-Sarthe
Sarthe

The small farm of the *bordier*, once extremely common in France, was the first to be affected by the great exodus from the land after the Second World War and the first of the second homes in France now numbering two million. The *bordier* farmed 3–6 hectares (7½–15 acres) of land often bordering a large farm and he paid tithes (*acensement*). He would keep a cow and a few animals so his cottage was often sited between woods and fields, where he could take advantage of common rights including the right to graze (*vaine pâture*) commonland, arable land, meadows and woodland. His house was simple: a byre for the cow, a single room for himself and his family, and a hay loft and store room over. He would have a work corner to pursue a money-earning craft and he would do seasonal work to help make ends meet.

Marais Vernier
Eure

The Marais Vernier is a large flat bay of drained marshland which once formed part of the delta of the River Seine. This great green expanse is contained by a sickle-shaped hillside rising up to a brow of thick woodland. Half-timbered farmhouses under reed-thatched roofs curve round the foot of this hill just above the level of the marshes. This is a typical Norman farmhouse, with its steep roof like the hull of a ship upside down and its hip roof at the windward end shaped like a ship's bow. Here, at the eastern, leeward end, where the cowshed is situated, a flight of steps, sheltered by a projecting half-hip of thatch, leads up to the *grenier* in the roof space. At the western, windward end, where the farmhouse is positioned, a single chimney sits astride the ridge at the end of a long line of plants, whose function is described on page 152.

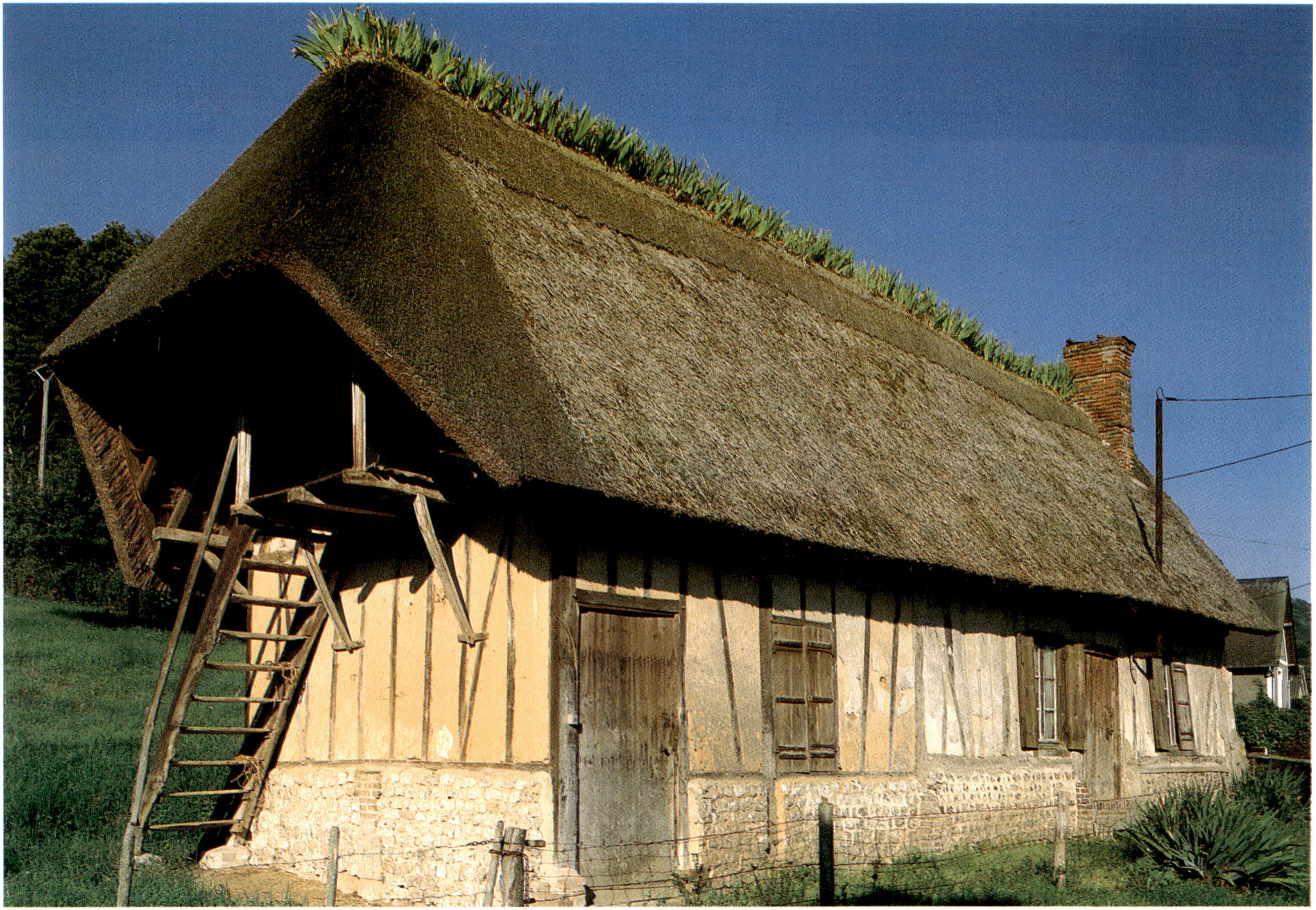

Marais Vernier
Eure

An eye-catching feature of the reed-thatched farm buildings of Normandy is the wealth of greenery growing along their ridges. The ridge is a point of weakness for the entry of rainwater, not least because thatch can slip down the roof over time exposing a gap. The solution used in Normandy is a capping of puddled clay mixed with chopped straw. Plants were established in this clay so that their roots could both bind the clay and lock the clay into the thatch. Iris is popular for this task because it has long fibrous roots and will tolerate the dry, hot conditions found on the roof. *Joubarbe* – 'stonecrop' – was also frequently used not only because it is at home in dry conditions but also because its French name means 'beard of Jupiter' and Jupiter is the god of lightning. People believed it would bring some protection from the lightning strikes which so frequently set fire to these highly combustible roofs.

Marais Vernier
Eure

The English poet Gerard Manley Hopkins must have included the Normandy cow in his thoughts when he wrote 'praise the Lord for dappled things'. Indeed, if this gentle cow had been included among Kipling's *Just So* stories, there is no doubt that her distinctive patterning would have turned out to be a consequence of spending her life in the dappled shade of Normandy orchards. She did this because the farms of this coastal region of Normandy were often set within an enclosed area of meadow land planted with fruit trees and defined by a hedge-topped earth bank called a *fosse*. The farm buildings were scattered about this enclosure, the animals would graze freely and the single-storey farmhouse – half-timbered and thatched – was placed separately on the northern boundary of the pasture to face south.

NORMANDY

Heurteauville
Seine-Maritime

Near the mouth of the Seine, on its southern bank, is this vast stone barn known as a *grange dimière*. It was built in the thirteenth century as a tithe barn for the Norman Abbey of Jumièges, which was founded in the seventh century and rebuilt in the tenth century on the opposite bank of the Seine. Originally given a tiled roof, the barn was thatched in the seventeenth century. Peasants had to pay *la dine* – one tenth of their produce – to the abbey, and this was stored in tithe barns like this. The church of the nearby Abbey of Saint-Wandrille was formerly a *grange dimière* at La Neuville-du-Bosc, which had been taken down and re-erected at the abbey. The farm buildings on the right adjoin the farmhouse pictured opposite.

Heurteauville
Seine-Maritime

These seventeenth-to-eighteenth-century farmhouse and farm buildings are ranged around the *grange dimière* and their light timber construction makes a strong contrast with the weighty stone construction of the great tithe barn. The closely spaced timber uprights give a vertical emphasis which is slashed almost haphazardly by the diagonal braces. Horizontal timbers are used to top and tail the timber frame and provide a common sill line to the windows and the first floor level. A dwarf limestone foundation wall raises this whole *colombage* – timber frame and lime-washed wattle-and-daub infill – out of the reach of rising damp. The roof above the jettied building on the left was covered in slate in the late nineteenth century at the earliest, whereas earlier, handmade, flat clay tiles roof the recessed building on the right. Both roofs would have originally been thatched.

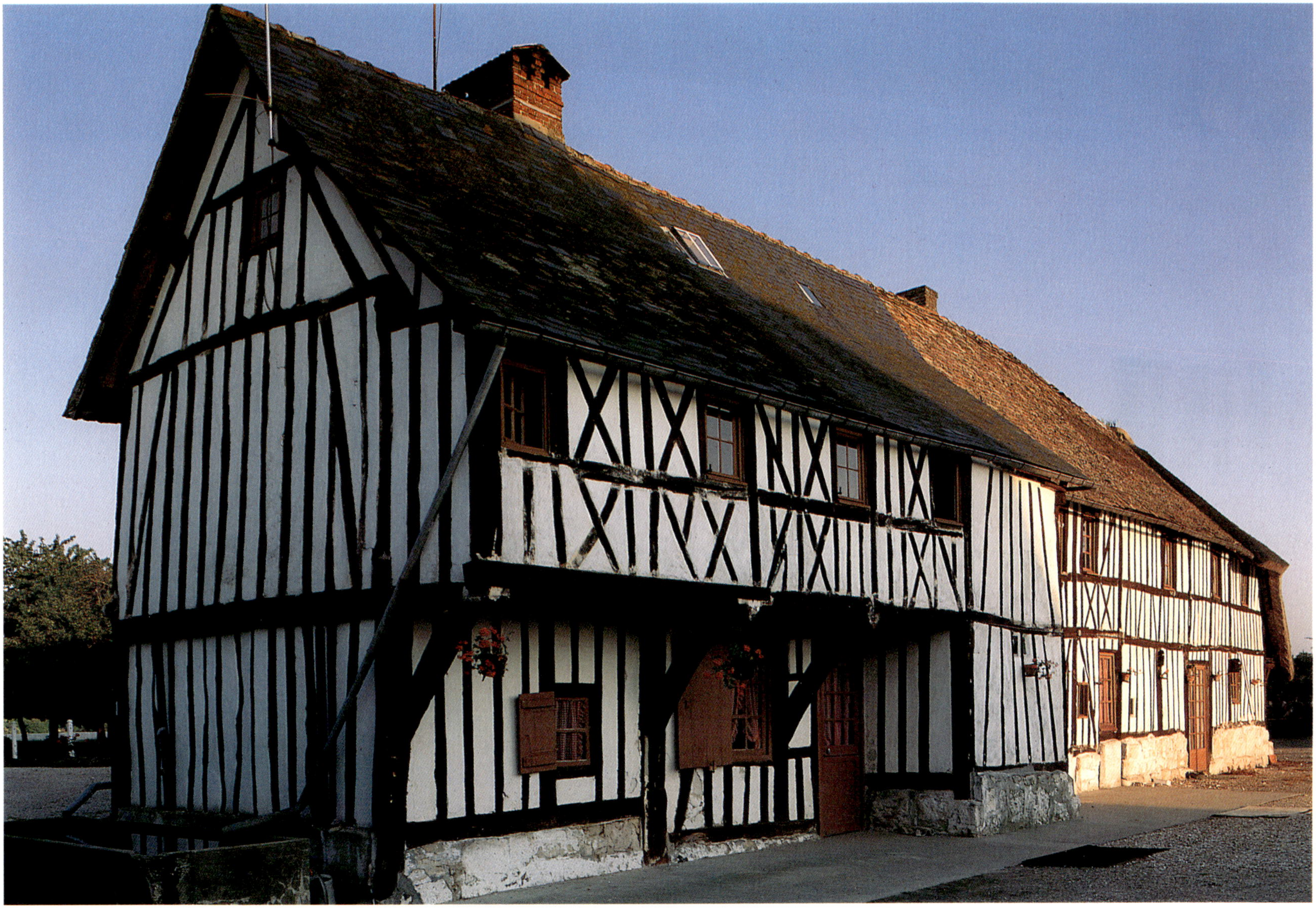

Glossary

Ancelle, anselle See **bardeau**.
Ardoise Slate tile.
Bardeau General term for a split timber roof tile (shingle). It varies in length from 330–450mm (1–1 ½ft) to 1–3m (3–10ft) and is mostly made from larch, spruce or pine but also from chestnut and less frequently beech or oak. Regional names include **essendole** in the southern Alps and **ancelle** or **tavaillon** in the northern Alps (**anselle** or **tavillon** in the Jura), where the shorter 330–450mm (1–1 ½ft) length is found, made from split spruce or pine and laid three to five planks deep.
Bergerie Barn for over-wintering and lambing sheep.
Bolet A covered porch or verandah.
Borie, cadolle, caselle, garriotte Regional names for dry-stone, beehive-shaped, corbelled limestone shelters found in Provence (**borie**), Burgundy (**cadolle**), Quercy (**caselle**) and Périgord (**garriotte**).
Cabane Name given to a simple one- or two-room rural dwelling from the Camargue to the Marais Poitevin.
Colombage A building, or storey of a building, comprising a timber framework (**pan de bois**) with infill (**hourdis**).
Coyau Name given to a flattening change of roof pitch at the eaves.
Croupette, demi-croupe A small or half-hipped roof, a hip (*croupe*) being a roof over a gable end of a house.
Essendole See **bardeau**.
Garriotte See **borie**.
Génoise A series of corbelled canal tiles (**tuiles rondes**) at the eaves which support a projecting roof; a feature of southern France.
Grenier Loft, granary or general food store, usually on the upper floor or in the roof space.
Houteau Rectangular or triangular opening in a roof made to provide the **grenier** with ventilation or light. Smaller and of less height and presence than a **lucarne**.
Hourdis Infill (wattle and daub) of clay or lime mortar (daub), keyed to a timber lath (wattle) in a timber-frame building.
Lambrissures Long planks of split timber hung vertically as wall cladding on farmhouses and farm buildings in Franche-Comté.
Lauze, lave Alternative terms for a stone tile of limestone, sandstone or schist.
Lauze d'Auvergne Stone tile of grey Auvergne schist.
Lucarne Dormer window.
Lucarne à foin Dormer roof projected in front of the opening below to support a pulley for lifting goods into the **grenier**.
Lucarne à la capucine Dormer roof shaped like the hood of a Capuchin monk.
Lucarne caussenarde Vaulted dormer constructed in the style of the stone vault architecture of the limestone *causses* of the Cévennes.
Mansard roof Roof with a double slope, the lower being longer and steeper than the upper; named after the French architect François Mansart 1598–1666.
Montoir An earth ramp to an upper level barn in the Massif Central.
Mortier de chaux grasse A lime mortar made up of one part slaked lime and two parts sand.
Outeau A small triangular roof opening providing ventilation and some light. Smaller than a **houteau**.
Pan de bois Collective name given to the horizontal, vertical and diagonal beams in timber-framed buildings.
Pas d'oiseau Literally 'bird steps' – a stepped gable wall, usually comprising stone slabs. Also known as **pas de moineau** (sparrow steps) in the Massif Central and the Pyrenees, and in Britain called 'crow steps' or 'corbie steps' (particularly in Scotland).
Pisé Building material made from clay mixed with water in a kneading process called puddling and used to construct external and internal walls and as an infill in timber-framed buildings.
Tavaillon, tavillon See **bardeau**.
Torchis Puddled clay, like **pisé**, but with additives such as 150mm (6in) lengths of straw to help bind it, fine gravel to stabilize it and cow dung to give adhesion. Known in England as 'cob', it is used to make internal and external walls and as an infill (daub) in timber-framed buildings.
Tout-venant Any small stones that come to hand for use in a wall between inner and outer skins of stone or between larger stones.
Tue, tuez Alternative terms for the great cone-shaped kitchens or chimneys found in parts of the Alps (Savoy, Franche-Comté).
Tuile de Bourgogne The original flat, rectangular clay tile (**tuile plate**). It was smaller than its successor and made by the Cistercian monks of Burgundy to cover their steep abbey roofs.
Tuile écaille 'Fishscale tile' – a flat clay tile with a rounded fishscale-shaped, bottom edge designed to lead rainwater into the centre of the tile and away from the joints between tiles. Also called *tuile en queue de castor*, or 'beaver's tail tile'.
Tuile flamande The pantile of northern France found in Picardy and Flanders. It was basically an adaptation of the two-tile **tuile ronde** system into one S-shaped tile.
Tuile plate A flat, rectangular clay tile.
Tuile romaine A clay roofing tile system introduced by the Romans and made up of an under-tile, a flat trapezoidal piece of clay made into a channel by turning its edges up, and an over-tile, also a trapezoidal piece of clay but half-rounded and with a wider diameter at one end than the other.
Tuile ronde Canal tile – a later adaptation of the **tuile romaine** system, where the half-round upper tile was also used as an under-tile the other way up.

Bibliography

Barozzi, Jacques, *Maisons et villages provençaux*, Ouest-France 1980
Bec, S. and Bruni, R., *Votre Guide en Lubéron*, Edisud 1986
Boucher, Michel and Furic, Joëlle, *La Maison rurale en Haute-Marche*, Édition Créer 1984 (eleven other regions published in the series)
Bouillot, Michel, *L'Habitat rural en Charolais-Brionnais*, Éditions Foyers Ruraux 1988 (also published in the series: *L'Habitat rural des origines au 16e siècle, au 17e siècle, avant la Révolution (18e s.), apres la Révolution*, and *L'Habitat rural* in eight other regions)
Braudel, Fernand, *The Identity of France: Volume One, History and Environment*, William Collins Sons and Co. Ltd 1986 and Fontana Press 1989
Braudel, Fernand, *The Identity of France: Volume Two, People and Production*, William Collins Sons and Co. Ltd 1990
Cayla, Alfred, *Maisons du Quercy et du Périgord*, Librairie Hachette 1973 (also published in the series: *Maisons du Normandie, Maisons de Bretagne, Maisons des Alpes*)
Cayla, Alfred, *Architecture paysanne de Guyenne et Gascogne*, Éditions Serg/Berger-Levrault 1977
Cévennes: Pierre sur pierre, Revue du Parc National des Cévennes nos 41, 42, 43, Revue Cévennes 1990
Champollion, Hervé, *The Story of the Brière*, Ouest-France 1989
Collection architecture rurale française, Éditions Berger-Levrault 1975–85 (volumes published for Savoie, Dauphiné, Corse, Alsace, Franche-Comté, Lyonnais, Midi-Toulousain et Pyrénéen, Bourgogne, Lorraine, Provence, Normandie)
Conseil d'Architecture d'Urbanisme et de l'Environnement du Nord, *Architecture dans le pays: Plaine de la Scarpe et de l'Escaut*, Dumoulin 1985
Construire en Queyras, Parc Naturel Régional du Queyras 1973
Coste, P and Martel, P., *Pierre sèche en Provence*, Les Alpes de lumière 1986
Deffontaines, Pierre, *L'Homme et sa maison*, NRF Gallimard 1972
Demangeon, A., 'L'Habitation rurale en France, essai de classification' in *Annales de Géographie*, No. 161, 1920
Demangeon, A., *La Définition et le classement des maisons rurales*, Denoël 1937
De Martonne, E., *Geographical Regions of France*, Heinemann 1933–58
Desjeux, Catherine and Bernard, *Les Parcs Naturels Régionaux de France*, Éditions Créer 1984
Doyon, Georges and Hubrecht, Robert, *L'Architecture rurale et bourgeoise en France*, Éditions Vincent Fréal 1957–70
Duchêne, Hervé, *Provence and its People*, Ouest-France 1981
Errath, C., Mar, D. and Le Quellec, J. L., *Le Marais Poitevin*, Geste Éditions 1991
Fillipetti, Hervé, *Maisons paysannes de l'ancienne France: 1, France Septentrionale*, Éditions Serg/Berger-Levrault 1979
Fillipetti, Hervé and Trotereau, Janine, *Symboles et pratiques rituelles dans la maison paysanne traditionnelle*, Éditions Serg/Berger-Levrault 1978
Forestier, Marc, *Secrets du Grenier Fort*, Marc Forestier 1985
Fréal, Jacques, *L'Architecture paysanne en France: La maison*, Éditions Serg 1977
Grillo, Paul Jacques, *Form, Function and Design*, Dover Publication 1975
Hansell, Peter and Jean, *Doves and Dovecotes*, Millstream Books 1988
Hermann, Marie-Thérèse, *Architecture et vie traditionnelle en Savoie*, Éditions Serg/Berger-Levrault
Houarn, Tal, *Maisons et villages bretons*, Éditions Ouest-France 1985
Jeanson, D. and Sarrazin, André, *Maisons rurales du Val de Loire: Touraine, Blésois, Orléanais, Sologne*, Editions Serg/Berger-Levrault 1977
Jourdan, Patrick, *Les Mas de Camargue: Analyse historique et socio-économique*, Édition de la Fondation du Parc Naturel Régional de Camargue 1987
La Maison de Bisping: Maisons paysannes de Moselle, Parc Naturel Régional de Lorraine, n.d.
Letenoux, Guy, *Architecture et vie traditionnelle en Normandie* Éditions Serg/Berger-Levrault
Malenfant, Pierrette, *Alsatian Open Air Museum: Ungersheim*, Éditions la Nuée Bleue/DNA 1990
Massot, Jean-Luc, *Maisons rurales et vie paysanne en Provence*, Éditions Serg/Berger-Levrault 1976
Meirion-Jones, Gwynn, *The Vernacular Architecture of Brittany*, John Donald 1983
Mounicq, Jean and Vallery-Radot, Nicole, *Les Toits dans le paysage*, La Maison de Marie Claire 1977
Pacqueteau, François, *Architecture et vie traditionelle en Bretagne*, Éditions Serg/Berger-Levrault
Ruch, Maurice, *La Maison alsacienne à colombage*, Éditions Berger-Levrault 1977
'Spécial mas de Camargue', *Courrier du Parc Naturel Régional de Camargue*, No. 33, Publication de la Fondation du Parc naturel regional de Camargue 1989
Stein, Annick, *La Maison dans sa région: Le nord*, Éditions Charles Massin 1991
Stein, Annick, *La Maison dans sa région: Les Vosges – La Franche-Comté*, Éditions Charles Massin 1990 (also published in the series: *L'Alsace, Vieilles Maisons normandes, La Provence, La Bretagne*
Trendel, Guy, *Le Guide des Vosges du nord*, La Manufacture 1989
Vandenhove, Jean, *Le Queyras: Villages et hameaux*, Office d'Information et de Promotion du Tourisme en Queyras 1984
Weiss, Walter, *Construire la maison: Les ABC de l'Écomusée d'Alsace*, Ministère de la Culture, de la Communication et des Grands Travaux, n.d.

Author's Acknowledgements

I would like to thank the following individuals and organizations for their willing help and information: François Joly, architecte, Cévennes Parc National; François Lalanne, Conservateur Chargé du Patrimoine, Parc Naturel Régional des Landes de Gascogne; Écomusée de la Grande Lande; Dominique Deviers, La Vanoise Parc National; Denis Raisson, Le Directeur Adjoint, Parc Naturel Régional Livradois Forez; Sylvia Hadland; Dominique Pierre, Parc Naturel Régional de Lorraine; Agnés Frapin, La Directrice, Conseil d'Architecture d'Urbanisme et de l'Environnement des Pyrénées-Atlantiques; Kit and Keith Turner; Madame Lassalas, Parc Naturel Régional des Volcans d'Auvergne; James Cox; Jean Bacon; Isabelle Bacon, Documentaliste, Parc Naturel Régional de Brotonne; Marie-Françoise Pees Martin, Fondation de France; Ian Mitchell: Étienne Lavigne, Architecte du Conseil d'Architecture d'Urbanisme et de l'Environnement des Hautes Pyrénées; Anne Kleindienst, architecte, Parc Naturel Régional des Ballons des Vosges; Parc Naturel Régional de Camargue; Emma Armitage; Parc Naturel Régional d'Armorique; René Mathé, architecte, Parc Naturel Régional du Marais Poitevin; Monique Lambert, Conservateur en chef de la Bibliothéque, Musée National des Arts et Traditions populaires; Philippe and Amélie de MacMahon, Duc et Duchesse de Magenta; Donald and Hélène Burrows; Monsieur J. P. Terrade, Le Directeur, Parc Naturel Régional du Pilat; Parc Naturel Régional du Haut Languedoc; John Miller; Parc Naturel Régional du Lubéron; Parc Naturel Régional des Vosges du Nord; Chloë, Rupert and Robin Walshe; Musée d'Offwiller; Parc Naturel Régional du Haut-Jura; Les Forges de Syam; Institute Français; Musée de Plein Air des Maisons Comtoises, Nancray; Écomusée Maison Michaud, Chapelle-des-Bois; Parc Naturel Régional de la Fôret d'Orient; Parc Naturel Régional Nord-Pas de Calais; Stephen Jenkinson; Parc Naturel Régional du Queyras; Barbara Mellor; Parc Naturel Régional de Brière; Colin Grant; Écomusée d'Alsace; J. Pierre Izans, Le Chargé de Mission, Les Pyrénées Parc National. In particular I would like to thank Carol Walshe and Elisabeth West.

Index

Page numbers in *italics* refer to photographs.

aisances, 53
Albi, 117
alpages, 113
Alps, 15, 21, 26, 28, 31, 33, 69, 85, 88, 113
Ambialet, Priory of, 115
ancelle or *anselle*, 72, 156
Ancien Régime, 11
Ankou, 33
Ardennes, 15, 29, 31, 49
ardoise, 29, 156
Argonne Massif, 50
Armorican massif, 148
Armorique Regional Park, 144
Arques, Pas-de-Calais, 45; *44*
Aurillac, 110
auvent, 123

Bages, Pyrénées-Atlantiques, 120; *121*
bardeau, 26, 156
Bar-le-Duc, 50
Beaujolais, 21
Beaumont-sur-Sarthe, Sarthe, 150; *150*
Bécherel, Ille-et-Vilaine, 23; *23*
Belgian brickmakers, 32
Benedictine monks, 45
Béon, Pyrénées-Atlantiques, 120; *120*
bergerie, 99, 113, 156
Bessans, 86
Beynac, Dordogne, 129; *128*
Bisping, Moselle, 53; *53*
bocage, 143
bolet, 119, 130, 156
Bonneval-sur-Arc, Savoie, 86; *86*
bordier, 150
borie, 97, 133, 156
Boulonnais, 18, 40, 43
Braudel, Fernand, 11
Bremontier, 123

Brière, regional park, 22, 138
Brotonne, regional park, 138
burons, 113

cabane, 35, 99, 135, 136, 156
cadolle, 133, 156
Caen stone, 39
Caesar, Julius, 22
Camargue, 35, 99
caselle, 133, 156
Caux, Pays de, 18
Caves Boeckel, 59
Cévennes, 21, 29, 31, 33, 101
Cévennes National Park, 101, 103
Champagnole, 74
Champsigny, Saône-et-Loire, 81; *81*
Chanticleer, 124
Chapelle-des-Bois, Doubs, 71; *71*
Château Biron, 126
Cistercian monks, 32, 45, 79
Clappier, Jean, 86
Col de l'Iseran, 86
colombage, 19, 56, 154, 156
Cotentin peninsula, 29
Coulon, Deux Sèvres, 135; *134, 135*
coyau, 126, 156
Crandal, Pas-de-Calais, 40; *41*
croupette, 35, 74, 156

Dagny-Lambercy, Aisne, 31; *30*
Demangeon, Albert, 13, 15
Doudeauville, Pas-de-Calais, 43; *42, 43*
Dutch Elm disease, 34

Ensisheim, Haut-Rhin, 64, 66; *64, 65, 66, 67*
épierrement, 133
Escaza, Lot, 119; *118*
essendole, 88, 91, 156
Etangs, Pays des, 53
eustandade, 123

Feast of St Urban, 69
Fontanes, Lot, 119; *119*
Forêt d'Orient Regional Park, 49
Forme d'Ambert, 109
four, 77
Fraisse-sur-Agout, Hérault, 25; *25*
Francis I, 81
Francis II, 138
French Revolution, 11, 39, 81, 115, 138

gardians, 99
garrigue, 97
garriotte, 133, 156
Genoa, 117
génoise, 94, 117, 126, 129, 156
Géraudot, Aube, 49; *48, 49*
Goethe, 63
Gordes, Vaucluse, 97; *96, 97*
Gouarec, Côtes-du-Nord, 144; *145*
Grande Randonnée, 110
Grandfontaine, Doubs, 69; *68, 69*
grange dimière, 154
grenier, 14, 39, 63, 117, 150, 156
grenier fort, 72

Hanau, 62
Haute-Maurienne, 85
Henflingen, Haut-Rhin, 62; *62*
Hesdin l'Abbé, Pas-de-Calais, 39; *38, 39*
Heurteauville, Seine-Maritime, 154; *154, 155*
Hofstede, 18
Hopkins, Gerard Manley, 152
hourdis, 49, 156
houteau, 63, 156
Hunspach, 60; *60*
huttiers, 135

Île de Fedrun, Loire-Atlantique, 138; *138*

Île d'Ouessant, Finistère, 147; *146, 147*
Imbsheim, Bas-Rhin, 58; *58*
Issigeac, Dordogne, 130; *130*

jas or *jasserie*, 109, 133
Jumièges, Abbey of, 154

kelsch, 66
Kerberon, Morbihan, 141; *141*
Kerhinet, Loire-Atlantique, 138; *139*
Kerlo, Loire-Atlantique, 14; *14*
Kérouat, Finistère, 144; *144*
Kipling, Rudyard, 152
Kochersberg, 56, 62
kratzputz, 66

Labergement-lès-Seurre, Cote-d'Or, 77; *77*
La Chapelle d'Abondance, Haute-Savoie; *1*
La Garette, Deux Sèvres, 136; *136*
Lajoux, Jura, 72, 74; *72, 74*
Lally, Saône-et-Loire, 81; *80*
lambrissure, 69, 71, 156
Lamoura, Jura, 72; *73*
Landes, 123, 124
Lascaux Caves, 133
Lauris, Vaucluse, 94; *94*
lauze, or *lave*, 31, 86, 91, 103, 105, 106, 109, 110, 115, 129, 156
Lavigerie, Cantal, 113; *112*
Le Bouchet, Puy-de-Dôme, 109; *108*
La Chau, Hautes-Alpes, 88; *89*
L'Ecot, Savoie, 85; *2, 84, 85*
Le Laus, Hautes-Alpes, 88; *88*
Le Pic, Dordogne, 129; *129*
Les Badieux, Lozère, 106, 107; *106, 107*
Les Bondons, Lozère, 105; *105*
Les Ecassas, Ain, 82; *82*
Les Eyzies-de-Tayac, Dordogne, 133; *133*
Les Forges de Syam, Jura, 74; *75*

INDEX

Lesmont, Aube, 50; *50*
Les Rayières, Doubs, 71; *70*
Les Viaux, Vaucluse, 21; *20*
Le Wast, Pas-de-Calais, 40; *40*
L'Héritier, Lot-et-Garonne, 126; *127*
L'Hôpital, Lozère, 105; *104*
Livradois Forez Regional Park, 109
logis, 99
Loire valley, 28, 32
Lubéron Regional Park, 35, 92, 94, 97
lucarne à foin, 50, 156
lucarne à la capucine, 141, 156
lucarne caussenarde, 105, 106, 156
Lyonnais, 21

Mâconnais, 21
Magenta, Duc de, 81
Maginot Line, 60
Mailly-le-Château, Côte-d'Or, 77; *76*
Manonville, Meurthe-et-Moselle, 53; *52*
Marais Audomarois, 45
Marais Poitevin, 135, 136
Marais Vernier, Eure, 150, 152; *151, 152, 153*
Maroilles, 31
Marquèze, Landes, 123, 124; *122, 123, 124*
Mas de Cacharel, Bouches-du-Rhône, 99; *99*
Mas du Pont de Rousty, Bouches-du-Rhône, 99; *98*
Massif Central, 21, 24, 25, 28, 82, 103, 113
Massif de la Vanoise, 85
Mauriac, 110
Mazod, 72
Meriadec, Morbihan, 143; *143*
Midi, 31, 90, 92
Mirandol, Tarn, 115; *115*
mistral, 35, 92, 94
Mittelbergheim, Bas-Rhin, 59; *59*
Monbazillac, Dordogne, 130; *131*
montagne and *montagnette*, 85
montoir, 82, 109, 156
Morey, Claude de, 81
mortier de chaux grasse, 143, 156
Morvan Regional Park, 81
Moulins de Kérouat, 144
Mulhouse, 64
Murat, Cantal, 113; *113*

Nancray, Doubs, 26; *27*

nez cassé, 31
Noiron, Saône-et-Loire, 79; *79*
Normans, 35
North Vosges Regional Park, 60

oeil de boeuf, 79
Offwiller, Bas-Rhin, 18, 54; *19, 54, 55*
Ordesa National Park, 120
outeau, 130, 156

pan de bois, 50, 156
panne flamande, 31, 43, 156
Paris basin, 50
Parliament of Paris, 81
Parranquet, Lot-et-Garonne, 126; *126*
pas d'oiseau or *pas de moineau*, 82, 105, 156
Pasteur, Louis, 101
pentwin or *penty*, 9, 148
Périgord, 29, 126, 130, 133
pierre à eau, 79
pigeonnier, 31, 39, 43, 92, 97, 99, 119, 126, 129
Pilat Regional Park, 82, 109
Piney, Aube, 50; *51*
pisé, 22, 24, 28, 53, 156
Plougrescant, Côtes-du-Nord, 9, 148; *8, 149*
Poillot, Denis, 81
potager, 46
Poul-Fetan, Morbihan, 143; *142*
Puy Mary, Cantal, 110; *111*
Pyrenees, 28, 29, 113, 120
Pyrénées Occidentales National Park, 120

Quatzenheim, Bas-Rhin, 60; *61*
Quercy, 15, 31, 90, 92, 119, 133, 148

Rabelais, François, 113
rastel, 103
Recques-sur-Course, Pas-de-Calais, 17; *17*
Regional Park of Nord/Pas-de-Calais, 43, 45
remembrement, 143
remues, 85
Ried, 64
Riquewihr, Haut-Rhin, 63; *63*
rognons de silex, 17
Romans, 9, 28, 33, 97, 129
Roussillon, Vaucluse, 94; *95*
Rudez, Cantal, 110; *110*

Runan, Côtes-du-Nord, 148; *148*
Saint-Bernard, Pas-de-Calais, 45; *45*
Saint-Cassien, Dordogne, 34; *34*
Sainte-Croix, Tarn, 117; *116*
Saint-Dizier, 49
Saint-Étienne, 82
Saint-Flour, 110
Saint-Genest-Malifaux, Loire, 82; *83*
Saint-Hostien, Haute-Loire, 109; *109*
Saint-Jean-Delnous, Aveyron, 115; *114*
Saint-Martin-de-la-Brasque, Vaucluse, 92; *93*
Saint-Omer, 45
Saint-Pierre-des-Tripiers, Lozère, 101; *100, 101*
Saint-Symphorien-sur-Saône, Côte-d'Or, 79; *78*
Saint-Véran, Hautes-Alpes, 90, 91, 92; *90, 91, 92*
Saint-Wandrille, Abbey of, 154
Schini family, 62
scraffito, 26
Serques, Pas-de-Calais, 46; *46, 47*
Sireuil, Dordogne, 133; *132*
Spain, tiles from, 31, 32, 46
Stothard, 22
Strasbourg, 56
Sundgau, 26, 66

Tarentaise, 85
tavaillon or *tavillon*, 53, 72, 74, 156
terre pétrie, 86
Thiérache, 31
torchis, 22, 23, 28, 40, 43, 46, 50, 64, 66, 156
tout-venant, 46, 103, 136, 156
transhumance, 11, 90, 99, 113
trésor, 72
Troubat, Lozère, 103; *102, 103*
Troyes, 49, 50
Truchtersheim, Bas-Rhin, 56; *56, 57*
tue or *tuez*, 71, 156
tuile de Bourgogne, 32, 79, 156
tuile en queue de castor and *tuile écaille*, 19, 32, 63, 66, 74, 156
tuile plate, 32, 43, 156
tuile romaine, 31, 156
tuile ronde, 31, 32, 156

Ushant, 147

Vallée d'Avérole, 86
Vallée de l'Aigue Blanche, 90
Vannes, Morbihan, 141; *140*
Vianges, Maquis de, 81
vigneron, 59, 130
Villandraut, Gironde, 124; *125*
Villefranche-d'Albigeois, Tarn, 117; *117*
Vincendières, Savoie, 86; *87*
Vitruvius, 22
Vitry-le-François, 50
Volcans d'Auvergne Regional Park, 110, 113
Vosges mountains, 29, 59, 63, 66
Vouillé, Vienne, 136; *137*

White Storks (*Ciconia ciconia*), 64

Zarbuli, Giovanni Francesco, 92